ADVANCE PRAISE

As the world gets exponentially more complex, the clarity necessary to make sense of the complicated is paramount. Entrepreneurism during this time of transition starts first and foremost with our inner journey to uncover and express why we do what we do. Jamie's words and clear metaphors through the lens of fencing helped make my path crystal clear to bring the next evolution of digital economics into reality. Great read to uncover your own inner greatness.

—RAY PODDER, FOUNDER OF GROW AND ON
NETWORK TO BRING REAL TIME CURRENCY
TO CONNECTED COMMUNITIES

Jamie's book is an exciting journey into how we can become better masters of ourselves. The process he introduces is at once fiercely logical and mystically intuitive. Our time working together has yielded key insights into my own hardwiring that have served as rocket fuel in my pursuit of personal and professional goals.

—JASON ROGERS—AUTHOR & OLYMPIC
SILVER MEDALIST IN FENCING

In On Guard and On Point, Jamie has created a unique way to access those "aha" moments in life that create clarity, so you can move ahead and accomplish what matters most to you.

In this profoundly enlightening book, Jamie expertly provides a roadmap for discovering what uniquely propels you forward at every stage of your life, showcasing how to balance being ON GUARD while remaining ON POINT!

As an entrepreneur and CEO, I like action...as Jamie took me from my Why to my How and finally to my What, I had a moment of clarity that immediately validated my gut feeling that I was on the right track in acquiring Mapconsulting. com. With his storytelling and challenging questions, Jamie's authentic voice connects, inspires and helps us make sense of why we think and act like we do...Bravo!

This well-crafted book will introduce you to a new way of seeing yourself from the inside out and will help you leverage your strengths, maximize your potential and create significant, lasting results in life and work. Jamie has a unique ability to connect with each and every one of us.

ON GUARD AND ON POINT

ON GUARD AND ON POINT

MASTERING THE DUEL BETWEEN LIFE AND WORK

JAMIE DOURAGHY

LIONCREST
PUBLISHING

ON GUARD AND ON POINT
Mastering the Duel between Life and Work

ISBN   978-1-5445-0432-2 *Paperback*
       978-1-5445-0433-9 *Ebook*

To Katty for your love, support, and patience while I was writing this book.

CONTENTS

"To be great in anything requires an enormous amount of will."

—PETER WESTBROOK, OLYMPIC BRONZE
MEDALIST AND SIX-TIME OLYMPIAN, USA

"Fight your opponent, not yourself."

—HEIZABURO OKAWA, THREE-TIME OLYMPIAN, JAPAN

"I felt so good today. I felt in a zone, and I knew I was going to win this...

There was no stopping me."

—MARIEL ZAGUNIS, TWO-TIME OLYMPIC GOLD
MEDALIST AND FOUR-TIME OLYMPIAN, USA

"Regardless of superiority or greater experience, no fencer can be absolutely sure of complete success."

—ALDO NADI, MULTIPLE OLYMPIC AND WORLD
CHAMPIONSHIP MEDALIST, ITALY

"I believe that we achieve things when we are ready to grab them."

—VALENTINA VEZZALI, NINE-TIME OLYMPIC
MEDALIST (SIX GOLD MEDALS), TWENTY-
SEVEN-TIME WORLD CHAMPIONSHIP MEDALIST
(SIXTEEN GOLD MEDALS), ITALY

"With my management and leadership experience on the national and international level of sport, also in business and politics and society, I am well trained for this great task."

"With sport, I have two lives. The first one where I became champion and learned a lot about myself. The second uses my passion to help others; sport is an incredible social remedy."

"I can tell you that if you are not nervous, if you don't feel that trembling, then you are not ready. When you are ready, there should be jitters. If you don't experience it, you lose!"

"Never be afraid of opportunities; always be on the lookout for adventures."

FOREWORD

BY DR. GARY SANCHEZ, FOUNDER
OF THE WHY INSTITUTE

"Can I just come out and help?" Jamie asked.

After having discovered his *why* and feeling its impact, Jamie told me that he wanted to see others discover and live their *why* and personally wanted to be part of that discovery process.

I met Jamie in 2013, while we were hosting a "Discover Your WHY" workshop in Albuquerque, New Mexico, for about fifteen businesses. The businesses ranged from dental offices to laboratories to insurance agencies and several others. The goal of the workshop was to discover the answers to three important questions:

- Who am I? (What is my personal *why*?)
- Who are we? (What is our business *why*?)
- What is our message? (How do we articulate our *why* to the marketplace to attract the right new clients?)

At the time, I hadn't yet developed the "WHY App," so we had to help the business leaders and their teams discover their *why* in one-on-one sessions. We worked individually with each person, asking them a series of questions to help them gain clarity into the driving force that had brought them success in their lives—that is, their *why*. These were very powerful and intense conversations that often led to wonderful aha moments—and even to tears in many cases—as participants discovered the words to articulate their *why*!

I could see Jamie chomping at the bit to help someone. He started out as an observer as he roamed the room looking for a way to be involved and make a difference. He listened intently to the WHY discovery process, then took notes and gave feedback, and you could tell he was preparing himself and learning. About halfway through the first day, I was looking around the room, and there was Jamie, over in a corner, working with one of the dental assistants, helping her discover her *why*!

There's nothing like the feeling of helping someone find clarity in who they are so they can move forward faster and have a bigger impact in their own life! Jamie realized this for himself in discovering his *why* and began experiencing the amazing feeling of helping someone else. I knew that the direction of his life had changed.

I had experienced that same feeling three years earlier when I was trying to figure out my *why*. I had heard so many experts and "gurus" talk about the power of knowing your *why*, and how it is critical in discovering yourself and accomplishing your goals. I desperately wanted to discover my *why* but couldn't find anyone who could actually help. Everyone was talking about it, but no one was helping me discover it. I became obsessed with finding answers!

I watched videos, read books, and worked with experts to help me narrow down the choices, and after eight months of hard work and self-reflection, I discovered that my *why* is "To find a better way and share it." Wow! That felt so right to me. My life has always been about finding better ways of doing things and sharing them, and until that moment, I was never able to connect the two.

I have inventions, patents, products, and trademarks that all improve on the way things had been done before.

Naturally, this led to the knowledge that I had to find a better way to help others discover their *why*! I developed a better process, so instead of requiring eight months and lots of hard, introspective work, I could help someone discover their *why* in about an hour. This process became the basis for the 9 WHYs and the algorithm for the "WHY App." This is the process Jamie learned so that he could help others discover *their why*.

As you will learn from the upcoming chapters in this book, when Jamie decides he is going to do something, he pushes forward until he reaches his goals. He knew that running his businesses in Los Angeles was not going to allow him to live his *why*. Instead, he committed to living a life of significance by helping others make sense of the challenges they face and discover their clear path to achieving positive results. As you will soon read, Jamie changed the course of his life.

He not only learned the processes I taught him, but in turn, he has also helped me to improve and expand the WHY Institute and has taught me a great deal along the way. *On Guard and On Point* will do the same for you.

FOREWORD

BY WARREN RUSTAND

Jamie and I met in November of 2011 and began a mentoring relationship. I am certain that I have learned as much from Jamie as he has learned from me. I know I gained a knowledge and feeling of joy from Jamie's success. We had fun tapping into capacity building for peak performance in the physical, emotional, intellectual, and spiritual areas of his life. We were learning more about life from immersion in life itself. This process was true "learning by doing."

To aide Jamie in his quest for success, we created a paradigm, within which the three most important principles of great leadership reside, ideas I have been speaking about for the past three decades. First, is Clarity of Vision. Second, Certainty of Intent. Third, the Power of Values.

Clarity of Vision is having a clear knowledge of where you are going. Certainty of Intent is acting on that Vision every day. The Power of Values is how we behave and live during the journey. Jamie came to understand these and applied them in all of his activities in life and work.

In all four areas of life, family, business, community, and self, Jamie taught me several wonderful lessons. He gave me insight into commitment, dedication, toughness, and resilience and moved to the next level. He did this by learning, applying, and teaching and continues that momentum still today. Once a person learns and applies correct principles to live in alignment with their values, there is no limit to one's potential.

Jamie continues to use these very principles each day, and now enables others to create greater clarity for accomplishment. This book is a compilation of the many lessons he has learned and now teaches from his own life experience. The book will allow you to gain knowledge and insight into your capacity to move to your next level and best self. To Jamie I am grateful and for you I am hopeful.

"One's success if relevant only when measured against one's own success."

—WARREN RUSTAND

INTRODUCTION

My goal for writing this book is to provide some concrete tools and exercises to help you find and implement your personal *why-how-what*. Many of these exercises are the result of conversations with my mentor, working closely with him to achieve personal goals as I trained for many a US national championship in order to qualify for the Veteran World Fencing Championships. The tools provided in this book are meant to serve as an entryway to discovering your personal *why*, determining your *how*, and realizing the impact of your *what*. It's a process that often works best alongside another person—an accountability partner. Once you connect with your *why-how-what*, and are clearly able to articulate your commitment, you become more focused and accountable when teaming up with someone else.

As I just mentioned, a key to growing with your *why* is your ability to clearly articulate it to others so that they can understand you. There will be prompts and exercises to facilitate these conversations. Readers who want a fuller learning experience can seek a workshop for further exploration or simply visit whyinstitute.com. At the end of the day, this is a book, not a person, and great things can happen when we connect with others!

Another objective is for you to experience mini moments of clarity as you read each chapter, gradually realizing what you're capable of and what more you can do with your life once you align yourself with your own *why-how-what*.

This book sums up my personal *why-how-what*. In it, I share with you what I learned on *my* journey of discovery.

My *why* is to contribute to the greater good. My *how* is to make sense of the complicated. My *what* is to create clarity.

What will yours be?

PREPARATION

An important part of being an entrepreneur is having a group of peers you can count on for open and direct feedback in times of transition. Since 2004, I've been a member of the Entrepreneurs' Organization (EO), a dynamic organization with thousands of members around the globe. At an event in Argentina, I reconnected with a friend I hadn't seen in a while. As we were going through our life updates, he mentioned he was working with a group that ran what he called "*why* workshops." I nodded with interest, however to tell the truth, I was more concerned about my updates than truly listening to what he was saying. When he asked what I was up to, I paid a little more attention to this subject and shared that I was still running my business while being increasingly unsure as to why I continued the day-to-day grind like an automaton without a purpose. I worried that the passion for the work I was doing simply wasn't there anymore.

His face broke into one of those understanding smiles people have when they can read you, and he said, "I can tell you *why* you are feeling this way in about twenty minutes."

His emphasis on the word "why" caught my attention, yet I ignored the moment and went into skeptic mode. I was quite doubtful. "I've been struggling with this for over two years, and you're going to tell me in twenty minutes *why* I've been struggling?"

"Trust the process," he said.

And so, I actually *listened* for the first time in a long time to someone other than myself.

He led me through an exercise, asking a series of questions concerning me and my work. I shared one story about what had made me feel successful at work and another about my personal life. His explanation was that there were 9 WHYs, and one of them was my hard-wiring. At first pass, this didn't make much sense to me. After asking some probing questions that I had to answer straightforwardly, he asked, "Do you often want to be a part of something bigger than yourself?" followed by, "If you do get the chance to be part of something bigger than yourself, how does that feel?"

Well, at that moment, I felt goosebumps! His analysis of

me was so spot-on that in an instant, I saw how all the volunteer work, fencing mentoring, and coaching I had done over the years was more meaningful to me than my day-to-day work because I felt successful when I helped other people. On the long flight home, I asked myself how I could best contribute to a greater good on a larger scale than with my company.

I decided to start by helping other people discover their *why* and became a certified *why* coach. Within a year, EO had invited me to run workshops around the world and facilitate sessions in Africa, South America, and Asia. In some workshops, even those where I needed an interpreter, I witnessed clear physical changes in the faces of the participants who connected with their *why*. Every time this happened, it gave me a great sense of fulfillment. When the participants provided feedback, they said that they thought I had been doing these workshops for years and told me I was a natural, which further reaffirmed that I was living in sync with what I had learned was my *why*. In a short time, I gained enough confidence in what I was doing to step away as president of the company that I'd been running for more than twenty years and set off on a new journey.

At a certain age, all kids want to know *why*: why they can't eat sugar-based foods all day, why they can't keep on playing when it's time to come home, why they have to go to school in the first place. As a matter of fact, the first thing most children ask when told no to anything is, "Why?"

Too often, the answer from the adult is simply, "Because I said so." Repeated over and over as a way of establishing control, this eventually led many of us as children to simply stop asking why. Some of us remember asking why often (a lot in my case) and being shut down time and again by an adult.

Children seek to understand their world as well as others in their world, and their persistent questioning comes from a genuine place of curiosity. As we age, we tend to stop asking why, even though it's a necessary, basic, and important question.

For a good part of my adult life, I followed one certain well-structured path, and in the span of a few short months, I chose to move my life in a completely new and totally different direction. For me, making a proactive choice was the difference between waiting for something to happen that would force me to change rather than making it happen on my terms. I felt energized with a renewed sense of purpose and a clearer understanding of my potential and what lay ahead. I finished a documentary, competed internationally in fencing tournaments, coached and presented around the world and wrote this book. I continue to work toward accomplishments that are meaningful to me—all at an age when many are thinking about retirement.

Stephen Covey's book *The 7 Habits of Highly Effective People* talks about how knowing our values helps us better define our *why*. Simon Sinek, in his TED Talk "Start with Why" introduced what he calls the golden circle: in the center is *why*, the next ring is *how*, and the final outer ring is *what*. He says we all know what we do, but we don't always know why we do it. With millions of views and counting, Sinek's successful talk and book of the same name have been a game changer for many.

Sinek says, "The goal is not to do business with everybody that needs what you have. The goal is to do business with people who believe what you believe"—that is, with people who connect with your *why*.

I have been a seeker with a curious mind most of my life. I began by reading selected works from a broad range of great thinkers and writers—Socrates, Marcus Aurelius, Nietzsche, Viktor Frankl, Alan Watts, and others. Over many years, I completed a series of personality tests—Myers-Briggs, DISC, CliftonStrengths, the Enneagram, and countless others. When I met Dr. Gary Sanchez at one of his WHY Institute workshops and learned how he distilled the broader *why* concept into the 9 WHYs, I was hooked. Next step was to become certified as a CliftonStrengths coach, which enabled me to dig deeper into understanding the importance of how we can maximize our individual strengths. Additionally, I became certified as a Conversational Intelligence Coach (C-IQ) to learn how to guide leaders to engage their followers via more effective conversations, as I learned from Judith Glaser that "our words create our worlds."

After helping people find their *why* in these workshops around the world, I realized that everyone wanted to learn more about making a better connection to their *why*, *how*, and *what*. That's because once we know *why* we do what we do, we need to know *how* to live in alignment with our *why* and *what* it takes to move in that direction. Once we combine our *why* with our strengths, we can create a powerful plan of action that leads to our having a greater capacity to do what we want to do. This moment of clarity led to my being able to discover the right combination and alignment of each individual's personal *why-how-what*, based on Sanchez's original 9 WHYs.

I saw this as a small way of furthering the collective body of knowledge that has been handed down to us over the centuries because once we know our own *why*, we need to know *how* to implement it and *what* to do. I believe that discovering our personal *why-how-what* is one of those micro aha moments that forms a part of our constant "search for meaning" (to paraphrase Viktor Frankl).

There is a visible shift when someone connects to the *why* of what they do. Some smile, some laugh, while others look dazed and astonished, their facial expressions and body language signaling their sense of discovery. While each person's response is unique, it is also remarkably universal—transcending language, culture, and background. Regardless of where I run my workshops, when dozens of participants discover their *why*, there are sporadic outbursts of applause and laughter. As people connect with one another and share their newly discovered selves, the energy of the room shifts from serious and focused to uplifted and energized.

Discovering your *why* creates clarity and leads to better communication in a relatively short amount of time. Clarity gives us a better idea of where we're going and our reason for going there. Once we know this reason, we can communicate with greater ease. When we are not clear on our direction, we move through life without purpose— laterally rather than onward and upward.

When we know the *why* behind what we do, we become clear on what we want and need for ourselves, as opposed to what someone else wants for us or needs from us. It becomes a lot easier to sift through the noise and determine where we should focus our energy. After a while, this noise becomes quieter as we learn how to turn the volume down. Otherwise, without knowing our *why*, we're constantly pulled in multiple directions, unable to focus on one thing long enough to gain traction.

> As humans, we tend to overcomplicate things and make up stories that sometimes cloud our clarity. If I can make sense of the complicated topic of discovering your *why* and help you gain clarity and take action, then I feel I am living in accordance with my *why* of contributing to the greater good. In turn, this feeling gives me more energy, which increases my capacity to take on more of what matters to me.

When I work with people who have never acted on their own *why*, they start with a lot of "I wish" statements drawn from their past. "I wish I had done this," or "I wish I had done that." Knowing your *why* gives you an opportunity to look forward to what you want to do next, how to get there, and why this is even important in the first place.

I decided that I didn't want to spend the rest of my life looking back on things I wished I had done. I wanted to look forward to what I could make happen next. There are thousands of well-written books that go down the path of giving advice on how not to let life pass us by. This is not that book. This is a forward-thinking book that focuses on the positive. Without getting too philosophical, I will only say that when you know *why* you do what you do, and how you'll go about doing it, there are no more excuses for delaying change.

The process of discovering your personal *why-how-what* will lead you upward to where you most want to be. The view is far clearer from well above the weeds!

CHAPTER ONE

ON GUARD

In fencing, much of the terminology comes from France, and *en garde* are the first words spoken by the referees to set the stage for the competitors, the fans, and themselves. These two words act like a trigger. Each fencer must now outfence the other, both channeling their energy and focus on scoring at just the right moment. It's French for "be on your guard" and essentially means "prepare yourself for what's next"—in this case, for beating your opponent or being beaten by that same opponent. To be on guard in fencing is to be prepared both physically and mentally, which is also a requirement for being ready for life. Before we do anything—accept a job, get into a relationship, buy a house, have a baby—we have to be ready. And we are most likely to succeed when we have taken the time to prepare. We have to know why we are trying to reach a given point, how we are going to get there, what we need to do once there, and where we want to go next.

For me, the sport of fencing is a metaphor for life. Before they even step on the strip, these athletes have made the commitment to show up and compete, and they know why they are there. They are physically and emotionally prepared to rise to the challenge, and what's beautiful about fencing is how it's all about the moment.

In a fencing bout, we experience two fencers battling it out, a referee calling the action, coaches shouting tactics, and fans cheering loudly for their athlete. On top of all this, fencing often feels like you're competing against yourself. Fencers have to think about their own strategy and preparation on top of figuring out what their opponent is trying to do to them. During a match, all the noise of life falls away, with the key to victory coming from building on a series of "being in the moment" moments, allowing the fencers to continuously access energy from within their exhaustive movements.

We all access this same energy when any project (major or minor) is being completed. When we're intensely focused on the present, little else matters, and what once seemed a very complex undertaking now feels simple. In other words, being in the moment truly matters.

When a touch is scored, the referee determines who established priority, and as fencers, we have to work hard to establish that priority. That's why fencing is a lot like living: if we don't know what our priorities are, we'll keep trying the same things over and over again to no avail. In life, the referee is our conscience, which keeps us in line, making sure we follow the rules and don't cheat. It also stabilizes us as we focus on our priorities.

Most of what we do in life is the output of our *why-how-what*. When we are in alignment with our *why-how-what*, we are better able to adjust to any circumstance and express ourselves uniquely and wholly. When we are not, knowing our *why* gives us an opening for change. If a fencer is not in alignment with any number of variables, that fencer can easily be knocked out in the first round. Tournaments last all day, sometimes two days, including long wait times. Fencers who arrive unprepared, or are mentally or physically out of alignment, go home within the first few hours, as they are not able to keep up with all that is coming at them in the moment.

Competing in a fencing tournament is akin to living a condensed version of life. Along the way, we have to make sure we prepare, hydrate, stay healthy, listen and learn from those who have been there before us and remain aware of our surroundings. Knowing your *why* helps you focus on what it takes to get you where you want to go and gets you back on track when distractions take you off track.

Far too often, we fall back on habits we know don't serve us well. Countless times, when I asked myself, "Why do you keep doing that?" it was because I didn't have clarity and didn't know how to change a given pattern, and I often asked that question in a negative, frustrated way—fraught with self-judgment.

Now that I'm clear on my *why*, if I catch myself going down a path I know doesn't serve me, I notice that the "there you go, you're doing it again" tone is different: it's without judgment. By being more self-aware, I can mindfully catch myself and note my behavior, free from negative self-judgments. Prior to knowing my *why*, it was much more difficult to catch such instances (because I had little self-awareness) and regain focus because the rabbit holes I would go down were so long and tenuous.

At my company, I worked with a senior account manager who excelled at sales. When I asked her why she worked in sales and what drove her to do a great job year after year, she said that she had been successful in sales because of her relationships that were strongly based on trust. She would do almost anything for a client if it meant they would trust her, and she would *do even more* once she knew they trusted her. This kind of drive isn't focused on outcomes so much as process. She was in full alignment with her purpose, so she could succeed at her job. Other salespeople on her team, who were less focused on process and more focused on outcomes, weren't as successful at providing excellent service. Eventually, they moved on.

When we know our *why*, we can easily see the gaps between what we're doing and what we really want to be doing. I call this being in integrity with oneself. Huge gaps or dissonances are an indication that we are out of integrity with ourselves, while alignments or resonances are evidence that our actions are in integrity with our beliefs.

Within an organization, when each of us is aligned with a specific function that fully complements our *why-how-*

what, we operate from a point of greater resonance. And the opposite holds equally true: the wider the gaps, the greater the dissonance. If employees are asked to fill roles that aren't aligned with their overarching reason behind why they do what they do, there will be increasing discomfort that can lead to job stress over time. People simply don't succeed at jobs and in corporate cultures that are not a good fit for them. For those who dread their work experience, their dissonance comes from not being in the right organization or in the right role, and this dissonance becomes louder as they ask themselves why they are there in the first place. This eventually spills over into other aspects of their lives.

As a board member of a nonprofit, I was asked to raise a certain amount of money each year, and if I didn't meet the goal through outside donations, I had to make up the difference myself. I was initially fine with that (or at least I thought I was) when I made the decision to join because I wanted to contribute. Yet somehow, I wasn't truly motivated to raise funds. I felt more strongly about bringing my skills and giving my personal time to make a difference versus using my time to raise money. I had joined the nonprofit primarily to raise awareness and help others—to contribute—and I interpreted "giving" as giving my time. After our third board meeting, dissonance set in. Suddenly, the reason I dreaded attending those particular board meetings became clear. It wasn't them. It was *me*! I needed a different environment in order to be able to serve, one more aligned with my personal *why*. I wasn't a good fit for that particular role on that particular board.

I believe that we are often a reflection of the places we frequent and the organizations we support. Knowing this, I've stepped up to serve on certain boards and stepped down from serving on others while searching for one that was I culturally aligned with my desire to have a positive impact.

The opposite of dissonance is resonance. The account manager whose story I shared earlier spent more than twenty years working in sales for one company because it completely aligned with her *why-how-what*. When our reason for living matches our role, we access that state of flow where work comes easily and joyfully. This is because we no longer have an ongoing need to question the work we are doing, or our place in it, and this mental freedom allows us to focus on what truly matters to us. When we live in integrity, we connect with other like-minded individuals who support one another in their growth without expecting something in return.

I now spend most of my time with the entrepreneurial, selected nonprofit, and fencing communities because, for me, these organizations and the people within them align with my *why-how-what*. I used to spend time with people who didn't share the same interests or values, and often felt that I was just hanging around while barely hanging on. I didn't realize that it was because of the dissonance between my personal *why-how-what* and their own *why-how-what*, plus the fact that we had no clear way to articulate what each of us valued. Because of that gap, I did not fully pursue the subjects or interests I wanted to focus on—the things that brought me joy. This resulted in a lot of wasted time for me and disappointment for those who expected me to deliver at a certain level.

When we realize our *why-how-what*, it becomes a lot clearer what or who brings us joy. Once engaged in activities that energize us, surrounded by people aligned with their *why*, we can be our best selves. We can easily get back *en garde*.

I now know that I thrive in certain communities, and because of this, I fully engage to inspire and impact others. An introvert by nature, I had rarely volunteered to be a leader until someone in the Entrepreneurs' Organization asked me to consider becoming the chapter president. What was interesting was to learn that others saw something in me that I wasn't aware of. And that one question, "Will you serve?" changed the direction of my life. I continue to serve and aim to encourage future leaders in the EO community to step up and lead.

Discovering our *why-how-what* leads us to connect our passion, purpose, and energy. Once we figure out why we get excited about a certain activity, event, or situation, we understand what drives our passion. The key is to concentrate on a purpose not just lose ourselves the passion. If not concentrated, our energy becomes like that of a little child: We run around all over the place until we collapse from exhaustion and soon discover that we haven't gone very far. We need to direct our energy toward what gives us meaning. Passion without purpose will eventually run dry. Too often, passionate people get drawn into work that doesn't energize them, and over time, their initial feeling of having a purpose gets overshadowed by a growing lack of alignment with how the work is being done.

Knowing what drives us is essential so we can develop personalized strategies for planning and mapping out our lives. What drives us to do X or Y or Z? What pushes us regardless of the outcome? Before embarking on any journey, we have to map out where we want to go. If we feel driven to play the piano, then we need to outline how we will get there and how we will measure progress along the way.

All of us have needs that vary greatly, are intensely personal, and are deeply meaningful. Looking beyond the physiological base of Maslow's hierarchy of needs, we all seek to uncover our core, which means getting out of the thinking brain (neocortex) and into the feeling brain (limbic system). If we can't determine why we do something, everything else becomes superfluous.

TO DETERMINE OUR DIRECTION, WE HAVE TO UNCOVER OUR CORE

- What do you want to focus on?
- How do you define yourself?
- What drives you?
- How would you define your priorities in life?

Once you know your core, seek out how to integrate it into your life more fully.

CHAPTER TWO

FOOTWORK

In fencing, good footwork enables fencers to move forward and backward fluidly. Without it, even a talented fencer won't succeed. Training starts with footwork because it is the foundation on which all other skills are built. Even when you launch yourself at your opponent, you still have to land on your feet. It's the same in life. We can go backward and forward, up and down, as long as we stabilize on the foundation of our *why*.

Dr. Gary Sanchez became curious as to how people

defined their own *why* and what was the meaning behind it all. At the time, there wasn't a clear definition or context to work with. Sanchez spent years talking with leading executives, doctors, coaches, artists, and authors. He gradually uncovered a series of patterns he called the 9 WHYs and identified that each of us is hardwired to follow a certain pattern. Of the thousands of people he queried, the vast majority expressed emotional connections to one of those 9 WHYs. Sanchez went on to found the WHY Institute to take his research to the next level.

Our *why* is internal and represents our hardwiring. It's what we respond to in the limbic brain. *What* is what we do. The *how* is how we go about doing anything and is closely related to our *why*. It's the bridge between our *why*, which is very personal, and our *what*, which is the impact we have on other people. *How* we do what we do makes each of us unique. The *how* is where our skills, strengths, and talents reside, and it's the manner in which we express ourselves.

In this chapter, we'll go through each of the *whys*. Later, we'll go to the next stages—the *what* and the *how*. Following are the 9 WHYs as described by Dr. Sanchez.

1. TO CONTRIBUTE TO A GREATER CAUSE

People with the "contribute" *why* feel compelled to be a part of something bigger than themselves. They love to support and enjoy the success of the greater good, the team, or whatever the cause may be. They are often found working behind the scenes, looking for ways to make the world a better place. When they are in a more public forum, it's to trumpet a movement or message they believe in. People with this *why* are go-to people, the ones you look for when you need help with just about anything.

Figuring out your *why* often means answering a series of questions. Here's how an elite runner from Africa, who had qualified for the 2008 Olympics, was injured for the 2012 games, and now 2016 was his last chance to run in the Olympics connected with his *why*:

When we spoke, I asked him why he ran. At first, he wasn't sure; then he decided it was for financial reasons. He needed to make money.

When I asked, "Why do you need to make money?"

He looked at me like I had forgotten rule number one in life and replied, "Because I need it to survive."

"Let's assume your survival is taken care of," I said. "Tell me why you want to make money."

After a few deep, thoughtful minutes, he said that he wanted to create a foundation and training center for runners in his home country. After digging a bit deeper, he confided that he only used to run when he was forced to as a form of punishment for misbehaving in school. When he acted up in the classroom, his teachers sent him out to run around the field; the greater the misbehavior, the more he had to run. Eventually, he realized that he enjoyed running and made the choice to become great at it. Running became the center of his life.

Over the years, running had taken him to the greatest sporting events the world had to offer, and now he wanted to teach kids the natural joy one gets from running. When I asked him why he felt compelled to start a track club in his community, he said, "It's important to contribute to others. It's absolutely imperative." That was his moment of clarity. That's when he connected with his *why*! Initially, he had considered training *and* starting a track club, now decided to focus first on his training, understanding that qualifying would help him to start a foundation in the future. He saw that he couldn't do both at the same time and that success in one area would bring him closer to living his main purpose in life.

Once we know our *why*, we create priorities that align with it. This frees us up to focus on what's really important to us and sets the basis for creating an action for getting there.

2. TO CREATE RELATIONSHIPS BASED ON TRUST

People with the "trust" *why* believe that trust is the most important thing in their life, and they will work hard to create it. They become educated as experts in a particular subject and demonstrate that expertise as a way of establishing trust. They do things "right" in order to demonstrate that they are trustworthy. They want to know that you believe in them and will go the extra mile to demonstrate this with their actions, words, and deeds.

A public relations leader in Los Angeles was known for bringing business leaders together with nonprofits. He had more than forty years of experience running his firm and would host people at his roundtables three times a day to foster a more close-knit community within the sprawling mass that is Los Angeles.

At a celebration for his company's forty-fifth year, he shared with me that almost every one of his client relationships was based on a handshake. He didn't see the need to draft up lengthy contracts. I asked how that was possible, given the modern-day business climate, and he said it was all based on trust. "If I trusted them, we would move forward. If I didn't, then the next handshake was a way of saying thank you and goodbye." For him, the handshake was the commitment, and there was little need for any complex paperwork. Those who knew him knew he was consistent and true to his word.

3. TO MAKE SENSE OF THE COMPLICATED

People with the "make sense" *why* observe, take in elements of every situation, and make sense out of them. They take complicated—or what appear to be complicated—factors, problems, and concepts and organize them to create solutions that are sensible and easy to implement. They are highly solution oriented and excellent problem solvers. They often use their skills to summarize complicated issues in writing.

A friend of mine became stuck while writing a complicated book on the future of global commerce. It was a huge topic, and he was having a hard time dealing with it. As we started talking about his issues, he realized his *why* was to "make sense of the complicated." The reason he wanted to write the book was that the world of commerce appeared to be overly complex, and he wanted to help people make sense of all the rapid changes. Remembering his *why* allowed him to revisit his book with a renewed sense of energy because once he was in alignment with his *why*, his writing and ideas began to flow unobstructed. He has now successfully branded himself as a sense maker, and is frequently invited to speak with leading global organizations all around the world.

4. TO FIND A BETTER WAY

People with the "better way" *why* constantly seek better

ways to do things. They can't stop themselves from "trying to do it better." They take virtually anything and want to improve it, make it better, and share their improvement with the world. As you discuss something with them, they are asking themselves, "What if we did it this way?" People with this *why* are constant innovators who create better processes and systems, are developers, and operate under the motto, "Often pleased, rarely satisfied."

A CEO in a large staffing company identified his *why* as "find a better way." As we walked to our cars after the workshop, he suddenly remembered a childhood incident. Growing up on a farm in Texas, his least favorite chore was pulling up those stubborn weeds from the family backyard. He was twelve at the time and recounted how his father had given him a small, not very sharp tool to uproot those seemingly immovable weeds. He recalled feeling upset by how time-consuming and inefficient doing it this way was and remembered saying out loud, "There has to be a better way. There just has to be!" This childhood memory solidified his *why* when he realized that finding a better way had been hardwired in him since childhood.

5. TO DO THINGS THE RIGHT WAY

People with the "do things the right way" *why* believe there is a right way to do things and that, if done at all, things should be done right. They neither cut corners nor skimp on details. They follow procedures, are results-driven, and believe that if the proper system is followed correctly, you will achieve the desired results. They believe in creating structures and processes for clarity, simplicity, and the correct running of operations.

One night, a group of us had dinner at a nice restaurant. As was his custom, the chef came out to sit for a while and discuss the meal with his guests. We asked him what it was like to run a restaurant and why he had started his own. He said he loved having people around and enjoyed making them happy through food.

"What about being a chef is important to you?" a guest asked.

After some thought, he said, "Well, every ingredient and every step has to be just right."

We asked him how important it was to have everything right, and he said, "Well, there is no other way!" He stated this with such emphasis that we all understood the underlying reason for the fact that his food always tasted so good.

For the chef, and for others with this *why*, everything has to be done correctly and attain a certain standard.

For him, it meant that the food had to be at the right temperature, served on the right plates, and set in the right atmosphere.

6. TO CHALLENGE THE STATUS QUO (CSQ)

People with the "CSQ" *why* think differently from those around them and challenge the typical way of doing things. They seek unique solutions that no one else has considered. They are extremely entrepreneurial and love innovation, particularly game changers. They look to create a market rather than to serve one. They often have a broad variety of interests. They may challenge you with comments such as "Why not?" and are often perceived as rebels—with (or without) a cause.

My sister is a photographer who uses an old-school Hasselblad 500CM with medium-format film. She recently received an invitation to do a photo shoot in Zimbabwe. Everyone—from our parents to her in-laws to her friends—was not supportive of the idea of her traveling so far by herself, yet for her, this was a dream opportunity. When she asked me what she should do, after much thought and knowing how important this opportunity was for my sister, I offered to travel with her as her assistant (it made complete sense to me at the time).

On the flight over, I suggested we go through her *why*. I

showed her the one-pager with the 9 WHYs. She quickly scanned it, pointed to "challenge the status quo," and said, "That's me." She insisted that she didn't need to spend any more time to go through the process. Knowing that we had hours and hours of flight time ahead of us and that watching movies, with our individual headsets on, wasn't going to bring us closer together, I pushed back until she finally agreed.

After about thirty minutes of sharing stories, many that I had never heard before, it turned out that she was right about herself. Her face and eyes lit up as she smiled broadly confirming her initial take on the CSQ *why*.

At the Great Zimbabwe ruins, she photographed a body-builder wearing a horned mask as part of her series on the Minotaur of Greek mythology as interpreted in an African setting. She snapped Polaroids to check the lighting before using the Hasselblad, and then, as she looked through the upside-down viewfinder of her Hasselblad and clicked, she burst out excitedly, "I just got goosebumps! That's one of the best shots I've ever taken!"

Connecting to her *why* helped remind her why she was on this trip; to challenge the status quo when it came to photography, to traveling based on pursuit of a passion, to classical mythology, and to tourism in Africa. Her book has now been published as a permanent witness to this journey.

7. TO SEEK MASTERY

People with the "seek mastery" *why* search for deep amounts of information over a broad variety of topics. They pick a specific subject and begin to learn about it, often for the sheer joy or curiosity of knowing something new. They gather and retain substantial knowledge in different areas. Typically viewed as "experts" in numerous disciplines, they insist that they have yet to truly master them. They are fearless about new subjects or ideas.

After my sister and I connected over discovering her *why*, I approached my eighty-five-year-old mother to try to determine hers. It was difficult at first because I was basing our conversations around what I remembered of her from my childhood and was jumping to my own conclusions. She was a teacher for forty years and very by the book. The first Fulbright scholar from her university, she now speaks five languages, even though she grew up in North Dakota speaking only English until the age of nineteen. Since then, she learned the piano, practices art, writes poetry, and possesses a library's worth of knowledge. She was a walking, talking instant Wikipedia before Wikipedia existed and can speak to countless topics. If she doesn't have the answer, she won't rest until she does.

She started yoga at forty and still practices at least twenty minutes a day.

When I finally asked, "How important is it for you to be good at what you do?" she replied, "Why would you do anything unless you're going to try to be good at it?" That finally triggered something, and when I showed her the detailed description for "mastery," she said, "That's me!" She was surprised to read something that explained what she had been doing her entire life without ever fully knowing why. She would undertake subjects and learn them very thoroughly until she reached a certain depth, at which point she would become bored and move on. When we all realized this, my father said, tongue in cheek, "No wonder she's been driving me crazy for over sixty years." He makes sense of things quickly and wants to move on from them, whereas she wants to go deeper into a topic until she feels she has fully understood it. They shared an aha moment that day, gaining more self-awareness even after six decades of marriage, proving that it's never too late to discover one's *why*.

8. TO CLARIFY

People with this *why* are always looking to be fully understood in all communications. They want to know that you get what they are saying and may find multiple ways of expressing a point. They will use analogies and metaphors to help cover multiple points of view on a particular topic that they are sharing. They feel successful when they know their message has been completely understood.

The CEO of a technology firm had an issue with a senior staff member, their head of technology who insisted on constantly tweaking everything instead of delivering exactly what the CEO had asked for. The CEO felt very frustrated and believed that he wasn't being listened to or even understood. After speaking with me for a while, I asked him how he felt about clarity.

"Oh, man," he said, "clarity is absolutely *everything!*" At that moment, he realized what he had said (rather loudly) and began to reflect on why he wasn't getting along with their head of technology. It was because the CEO wanted a clear understanding of what he would be receiving while his techie (whose *why* later turned out to be "find a better way") would never deliver on what he had initially promised, as he kept on changing and fine-tuning the deliverables. At that moment, the CEO realized his intense focus on clarity meant that he needed to find a more effective way to communicate (versus repeating himself) to his team in order to get them to do what he needed them to do in a timely manner.

9. TO SIMPLIFY

People with this *why* take a task that needs to be done and before tackling it, break it down into its simplest form. They remove unnecessary elements and streamline as a matter of course. They eliminate complexity in everything they do, which benefits themselves and everyone else.

Occasionally, discovering someone's *why* can be a very emotional process. I was being treated for an injury at a sports doctor's office and noticed how everything there was neatly arranged. I was curious to know if the doctor was driven by the need to do things in a certain way. She and I spoke at length about her practice, and when I eventually asked, "How important is it for you to simplify?" She looked quite moved, saying that simplification was extremely important. "What about this importance is causing strong feelings?" I asked. She said, "I thought I was almost bordering on OCD, because I constantly arrange things both at work and at home."

I asked about the feelings again, and she replied that her husband's things were strewn all over the house in disarray. "It drives me nuts that I have to keep rearranging everything," she said. Once she read the *why* of "to simplify," she felt a huge sense of relief. By understanding herself and her natural desire to have things in order, she could embrace this and focus on what she was great at.

The runner whose story I shared earlier was introduced to me by this sports doctor. The two were working together while he trained for the Olympics, and they had been butting heads, having a hard time aligning around a specific training and health regimen. After we had gone through their *why-how-what*, we found that his *why* was "to contribute," his *how* was "trust," and his *what* was "to find a better way." In comparison, the doctor's *why* was "to simplify." Her *how* was "trust," and her *what* was "to do things the right way."

Since he was so eager to contribute, he would say yes to any request for his time, even if it sapped him of his energy, and as his *what* was to find a better way, he was often experimenting with many new ways to train. This frustrated the doctor, who aimed to simplify her client's life by urging him to make fewer commitments and do things the right way by following a trusted and proven process. Since they depended on each other to get to the Olympics, identifying their personal *why-how-what*, and seeing that they both shared trust as their *how*, they changed their conversations and this helped them figure out what was misaligned in their professional relationship.

The doctor's ability to simplify helped the runner identify what was actually worth his spending time and energy on and what took away from his training program and achieving his goal. He realized that taking on more responsibilities moved him further and further away from winning a gold medal or even from qualifying. Building your personal *why-how-what* is best done in tandem with another person. When we know our *why*, or what drives us, we can align with the people we live and work with. We learn to understand the reasoning behind someone else's actions as well as what lies behind our own. Knowing our *why* helps us to make better decisions and to more clearly communicate the thought processes behind these decisions.

When we have clarity, we make more informed and educated decisions. Many of us make choices and wonder why we ignored our gut, and instead chose to do something else or nothing at all and the opportunity passed us by. More often, knowing our *why-how-what* can help us catch ourselves before we make a misstep.

At each turn, we can ask ourselves, "Is my decision in alignment with what I believe in and with my *why*? Do I know how to do this, or handle this, in the best way possible?" These questions provide a structure and process for obtaining clarity and ensuring that we make the right decision at the right time.

Ultimately, aligning with our *why* brings us joy. When the doctor has a neatly organized home, she feels great. When the runner gives back to his community, he feels fulfilled. When my mother is mastering a language, she feels like her best self. Living in accordance with our *why* makes us feel good, gives us a healthy dose of oxytocin, and when we feel our best, we want to continue to live that way. It becomes cyclical in the most positive of ways.

In fencing, we always come back to the *en garde* position to begin our footwork. The knees are comfortably bent, the back is straight, and the center of gravity is primed to move in either direction as needed. Fencers look and feel solid. They're able to move with ease, always returning to the same central position. The Why Stack, which is built on the foundation of our personal *why-how-what* (which will be discussed later), like the *en garde* position, is stable and supple. When we are aligned, we are consistent, strong, and grounded.

CHAPTER THREE

PARRY AND RIPOSTE

In fencing, a parry is a defensive move. A riposte is
the offensive response that quickly follows. It's akin to
blocking and attacking, as these actions establish "right
of way." It's a physical back-and-forth that mirrors the
back-and-forth we deal with mentally on a daily basis.
Humans negotiate with themselves constantly. When we
have to make an important decision, we weigh each side
and ask ourselves, "Should I do this? Should I not do this?"

Sometimes we get so caught up in the debate that we end up doing nothing.

When you fence, you have to do *something*. If you don't, you'll get hit. If you just stand there preparing for even a millisecond longer than is necessary, your opponent—being better prepared at that moment—will strike! Life is similar: we must not stand still waiting for things to change or happen and not take action. We have to be proactive in order to move up to the next round and be fully prepared for that next challenge.

Oftentimes, a fencer needs to move back in order to give themselves some distance apart from an overbearing opponent. Those steps back are not passive moves. They are proactive. Without controlling that space between the two, they could easily get hit. And just as good footwork is important in terms of advancing and retreating, the back-and-forth exchange of a parry and riposte are successful when completed as a whole. Without the block or parry, there cannot be the riposte or response.

In life, the mental back-and-forth usually occurs between a challenge and finding the way to meet it. That feeling of being stuck becomes a problem when we don't do something about it. We have to face down that situation if we don't want it to become an even bigger challenge. Pulling back in life can be good as well, as that space allows us a moment to reflect on what is truly needed to help us move upward faster. Simple breakaways, such as taking a walk or scheduled time to reflect, are easy and efficient examples of pulling back for brief moments during our busy periods that are too often overlooked.

At five foot six, I'm not tall, and I often encounter fencing opponents over six feet. It's a challenge for me to manage the distance between their longer reach and my shorter one. Unless I overcome this, I will quickly fall behind on the scoring. I need to be clear on my objective, "win the bout"; clear on my strategy, "control the distance"; and absolutely clear on my action, "score the next touch."

A challenge in some people's lives could be their current weight or their financial situation. Either of these may be manageable at first by cutting out certain foods or cutting down on certain expenses, yet if they continue to eat unhealthy foods and avoid consistent exercise or if they fail to practice fiscal discipline, they may soon find that they have gained even more weight or fallen even further behind on their financial objectives. What started out as just a challenge becomes a major problem.

A challenge becomes a problem when we don't do anything to address it, and instead, we simply repeat learned patterns of behavior that may buy us some short term time. Inevitably, this so-called bought time runs out because the precious commodity of real time, once lost, can never be recovered. At that point, other pressures start to really weigh in, and we find ourselves surrounded or trapped by the negative side of life.

In a fencing competition, the challenge is clear and right in front of the fencer: beat the opponent. Without training based on a well-thought-out and well-developed plan, the fencer lacks the confidence needed to execute physically and mentally demanding moves. Getting the right training in advance is an integral part of the overall plan to win. Without the right training, the fencer can't access the right mindset to score the next touch, let alone win the match.

In life, an ongoing challenge is feeling stuck at a particular stage. The way to meet this challenge is to have a plan beforehand for becoming unstuck and implementing it over time as the need arises. Otherwise, the plan itself is simply a nice idea with no value in the absence of execution.

We need to understand why we feel stuck. Without knowing our *why*, we can't create a plan of action through our *how* and *what*. While at first these may seem like separate steps, much like the parry and riposte, the success of the *why-how-what* is heavily dependent on their connection. Once people have identified and connected with their *why*, they want to know *how* to implement it and *what* to focus on. The answer was in the 9 WHYs and the creation of the Why Stack.

We operate at our best when our *why-how-what* are in alignment, as this provides the clarity we need to focus on what we care about the most. We now can more fully access the energy we actually have and can thereby increase our capacity to achieve our goals. Pulled in a hundred different directions each day, this configuration can simplify our lives in order to know where to focus our energy.

Those of us whose *why* is to contribute feel a need to help so much that oftentimes, when asked to give, our immediate response is "Yes." What I have learned is that by saying yes to most any opportunity to help someone, I was in fact saying no to what really mattered to me. I found myself overcommitted and pulled in too many different directions, always wanting to lend a hand. I now say yes only to the things that truly matter to me. In order to best function and flow, we need to hone in on fewer actions that better align with our *why-how-what*.

When we discover our *why*, we create a foundation for understanding ourselves better. Lacking this basic understanding, it can be hard to know what to focus on. Once we establish how we need to proceed, we need the discipline to stick with it.

Success is often the result of the level of self-discipline a person needs to attain combined with their capacity to take on the challenge itself. The extent of one person's capacity may be enough to win a regional or national tournament, while another person has the capacity of a professional athlete to perform at the highest levels in the world. Discipline doesn't always come naturally. It's a result of concentrated hard work on a specific task—in one word: effort. In fencing, this means performing the same moves over and over, gaining precision with small adjustments. In our lives, it means often missing out on dinner or events with friends or family and working on our craft instead. It means getting up when everyone else is still asleep in order to honor that commitment well before the workday begins.

For example, my *why* is to contribute. *What* I do is to create clarity, and *how* I create clarity is to make sense of the *complicated*. My *how* is predicated on the level of discipline I have because without discipline, my energy and attention would be scattered. This book is an example of living in alignment with my *why-how-what*. I wrote this to contribute to the greater good, and I planned on doing so by creating clarity around the process of identifying and expressing our unique and individual *why-how-what*.

In order to write this book and make sense of a complicated process, I needed to put in the hours it took to outline, draft, revise, and rewrite over and over. Without discipline, this book would not have been written, the process would not be fully clarified, and people who wanted to better understand why they do what they do, and how they go about doing it, might still be searching.

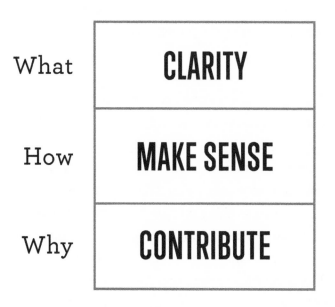

What	CLARITY
How	MAKE SENSE
Why	CONTRIBUTE

Eventually, as it evolves into more of a flow, discipline becomes a good habit, fully integrated into your life. Rather than "Fake it till you make it," which is disingenuous, you move your mindset toward "Work at it until you become it." I find this mindset to be more authentic, and how that manifests depends on the individual's work ethic.

Once you know your *why*, you can revisit projects you

have committed to with a new perspective and ask your-self, "Does completing this project bring me closer to or further from my goal?" When the answer is "closer," you are on the right track and in alignment with your inner self. If it's "further," then what better time than at that moment to have a long-overdue inner conversation and free yourself from the burden of carrying on with some-thing you are not truly aligned with?

Along the way, it may be that people in your life will dis-rupt your progress and distract you from your goal. If you want to write, the phone will ring or the kids will want something, and it becomes important to keep distrac-tions from annoying you and figure out how to respond and continue pushing through in a constructive manner. It's the same in fencing, where the fencers change tactics, beating the blades aggressively, parrying and riposting all over the strip, each setting the other up to fail because each one wants to win. Having the discipline to continue—despite any distraction—is crucial.

Discipline is essential, as it allows us to avoid the stopping and starting that happens with our many projects and undertakings in life. It helps quiet our screaming monkey brain that wants to run off and do something else. Oth-erwise, inconsistency in our activities cancel each other out as we hop from idea to idea from one side to the other, keeping us much closer to that starting line, than bringing us closer to the finish line off in the distance. Finish what you start and start what you can finish.

How much of our lives is the accumulation of unfinished projects? The unfinished book, or the semi-completed paintings lying around gathering dust or the half-done business plan? When we don't know *why* we pursue a project, we often lose steam and move on to the next thing that appears new and interesting for that moment. When we engage with projects that are in alignment with our personal *why-how-what*, we are better able to stick with them for the long term, as completing each step brings renewed energy.

For a CEO I spoke with, it was writing. I asked how long it had been since he had written, and he said ten years. "What kept you from writing?" I asked. He said that he had no idea. When he discovered his *why*, all that mattered from then on was that he returned to writing and no longer made excuses.

How many of us are stuck in that same mindset? What will it take to become unstoppable and act on what we should be doing?

When we repeatedly neglect the work we want to do (and make excuses for not doing it), dissonance sets in. Once we step out of alignment with ourselves, combined with more passing time, the wider the gap becomes. We are all guilty of this, and the choice to make is whether to put energy into dwelling on something we should've, could've, or would've done but didn't do or to put that same energy into moving forward and upward.

Motivation, discipline, and determination play their own roles in this process, with discipline acting as the connecting bridge between motivation and determination.

During a patch of time when I was struggling to keep a consistent training regimen, my mentor shared a very insightful thought: "Discipline doesn't care; discipline does." With discipline, we strive to complete whatever it is we are determined to accomplish, as opposed to only doing what we feel motivated to complete. Motivation gets us to that starting line. Determination gets us over the finish line, and everything in between is an effort.

At the age of forty, I set out to complete ten marathons, one a year for ten years. From the outset—and over time, several marathons into my personal goal—I continued to be motivated to run those ten marathons. Yet I fell short of my goal. I finished only seven. What happened?

The seventh marathon was in Chicago, one that I was going to complete with my two brothers. It was the thirtieth anniversary of the Chicago Marathon and one of the hottest on record. It was so hot that unknown to us, there was a heat-related fatality, and they had to shut down the race halfway through our running pace. Earlier in the day, our parents came to cheer us on, and as we turned a corner near Wrigley Field, we could see them in the crowd. In one of those moments that freezes time, the look on my father's face, with tears of joy streaming down his face at seeing his three sons sharing a memorable moment together, struck deep. Hours later, our parents were at Buckingham Fountain near the finish line to meet us and to make sure we survived the ordeal. We were tired from running yet high on the adrenaline-infused energy that accompanies sharing a life event together. It was an emotional day for all of us. In my heart of hearts, I believed it would never get better than that moment.

With my *why* being to contribute, bringing us together made me feel like I had contributed to a greater good for our family—in this case, the happiness of our family. My *what* is to create clarity, and *how* I create clarity is to make sense of the complicated. Coordinating the details of the trip and syncing up our training and diet regimens aligned with my *how*, which in turn provided the clarity needed to develop the right mindset to complete those wrenching 26.2 miles. As much as I used the earlier example of my personal *why-how-what* showing up in my writing this book, it manifests just as strongly in my personal life. The intersection of life and work is strongest when these three align.

After the three of us crossed the finish line together, we celebrated, hobbled home, and jumped into our ice baths to begin the physical recovery process. Coming together created an energy that felt exactly the same as when we were three little brothers and had to share bath time together more than forty years ago. Although I had set a personal goal to run ten marathons, I now no longer had a compelling reason or the motivation to meet that goal. Emotionally, I fulfilled what I had set out to do (challenge myself) and simply did not have the determination in this instance to see the other three marathon races through.

That's what I mean when I say I believe that motivation is emotional. It's driven by an emotion, whether or not we specify it. Motivation, like emotion, comes and goes, while determination stays once you set your mind to it.

Sometimes it's okay to leave projects unfinished, as long as there are no regrets and they no longer align with your goals. However, if you have a strong enough twinge of regret about something you have left unfinished, go back to it, pick it up, and see it through to its completion. If not, move on.

Goals that we commit to need to be within our capacity.

Otherwise, we won't reach them. There's a tension that happens when expectations don't meet reality, so it's important that the two align. Especially when you put a plan together, be real and be true to yourself. Having it all and doing it all is a fallacy. We don't need to do everything. We need to focus on what truly matters in our lives and what we can realistically accomplish. "Doing it all" is a well-marketed, often overinflated, and over-messaged dream to get people to do more and consume more than what is really needed in order to feel fulfilled.

REVISIT A NEGLECTED PROJECT

- What's the one project that you stopped working on and want to revisit?

- Why that particular project and why revisit it now?

- What's the one project that you are willing to walk away from and close out for good?

CHAPTER FOUR

THE MENTAL GAME

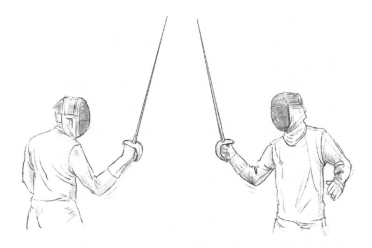

At the 2016 Olympic Games in Rio, I watched these elite fencers ready themselves for their upcoming bouts. Instead of strutting or pacing, they either bounced lightly in place from left to right, much like a boxer does, or remained still. Since fencing is a combat sport, the best fencers are the ones who find a way to remain calm during the heat of the bout. Externally, they may portray a level of intensity, yet internally, their minds are quiet and focused. Before a match, they visualize successful moves or meditate to clear their minds. *They don't rehash past victories or defeats.* They focus on preparing themselves for the only moment that matters, the upcoming "now."

Olympians prepare a lifetime for their moment of a lifetime. They reach the Olympic Games because of their commitment to how they start each day and what they spend that day doing. As with all activities that require concentration, fencing is a particularly mental game. It doesn't depend on weight, class, or age. It doesn't matter if you are a child, a young adult with parents in the stands, or a fifty-something with your own children in those same stands. Everything is about the moment. The internal mindset must be the same for every competitor who wants to win. Those who don't have their mental game together won't have a chance at winning.

In both fencing and in life, people are going to surprise you and catch you off guard. As a fencer, your opponent is always trying to trap you in that one crucial moment, while you're working away at doing the same to them. Creating a proper mindset ahead of time allows fencers to adjust quickly to unplanned events or situations. What separates excellent fencers from the rest is having a plan. What helps them move to the next round is being able to adjust to the unexpected.

This mindset isn't the exclusive domain of fencers. It's all around us when people engage in their craft. For example, in business, it is often the entrepreneur who possesses an uncanny ability to shift gears quickly, especially when they recognize that their plan isn't working. That doesn't mean abandoning the plan; it means going back to the foundation—back to their personal *why-how-what*.

Ultimately, there are only three things we can control every day: our minds, the right use of our energy, and our time. When we control the state of our mind and what we focus on, we control our energy. In the same way that athletes warm up their bodies before they practice or compete, we need to warm up our mind at the start of each day, knowing that this will enable us to determine what we focus on, control how we use our energy and how we optimize our time.

How we start our mornings sets the tone for the rest of our day. Unfortunately, many of us currently start up our brains by turning to a digital device to check the news, text messages, unread emails, and social media updates. The glowing tablet in the dark is a beacon that draws us in. Like a deer in the headlights, we stare at the oncoming vehicle and don't move. What a way to start anything— with a habit that simply isn't good for us! Reading about another international crisis or the passing of someone's loved one is a shock to the brain. It's rare that any good news or some nugget of truly valuable information arrives in the early morning, given that at any time of the day, news is mostly negative. It's like jumping into an icy lake in winter. The cold takes your breath away.

Athletes understand the importance of clearing their minds. Tennis players are often seen examining or readjusting their strings, even though there's not much to adjust. It's more about getting their mind ready for what's to come. Fencers bend their blades, check out their tips, or adjust their masks. These are the brief rituals athletes follow to recenter themselves.

When we open our day with a digital device, we don't give ourselves that opportunity to recenter. Instead, we start our day somewhat off-kilter.

Knowing we can control our mind and our time, we can choose to postpone dealing with all that digital noise to a scheduled moment during our day. We can decide when we are truly ready for the noise by creating or choosing different ways of waking up to the world.

Here's one way to wake up to the world that has worked well for me over the years: The 10-10-10 Exercise of Reading, Thinking and Writing—learned from my mentor who has successfully coached *Fortune* 100 CEOs, top athletes, and global leaders.

THE 10-10-10 EXERCISE: A SIMPLE THREE-TIERED PROCESS

- Ten minutes of reading great thoughts of others
- Ten minutes of reflecting on those great thoughts
- Ten minutes of writing your own great thoughts

It's a relatively quick exercise that's akin to a mental warm-up. Before we tune into the noise of the day, we can prepare and center ourselves. I tend to read books that will help me learn and grow. It could be a classic novel, a self-awareness book, or a graphic novel. Ultimately, we need to read something uplifting and positive to start our day.

A time of reflection, just as it is for the boxer about to enter the ring, is a time to clear the mind and think about what it will take to create a personal win for the day. I prefer to reflect on what's important to me and what I can do that day that will bring me closer to my goal. What will I do to keep me in alignment with my personal *why-how-what*?

The ten minutes devoted to writing can be used to brainstorm or to write in the style of Julia Cameron's "Morning Pages" or to write with a prompt from someone like Deepak Chopra. Ideally, this is done by hand. There's a physicality to handwriting that helps warm up the mind and inspire a tendency to own what goes onto the page, even if we decide to adjust the thought later on. It's far too easy today to hit the delete key or edit on the fly while we tap away on our keyboards, forgetting what we have just written, as oftentimes the words are selected for us.

When our minds are calm, we can go through the process of understanding our personal *why-how-what* and connect it to the day-to-day in a more deliberate manner. Clearing our mind leads to seeing the difference between reacting spontaneously and responding thoughtfully. Reacting may take us further from our goal, whereas responding can bring us closer because we don't always know the consequences of a reaction that hasn't been fully thought through. Do we want to spend our entire day reacting or being clear in our response?

When I decided to aim for a national championship in fencing, I knew that I needed to change my daily habits. I decided to wake up an hour earlier each day to train, and I started each morning intentionally going through the 10-10-10 Exercise. By planning it out, I knew exactly what I needed to do at a specific time and controlled my time to maximize my energy and focus. After seeing great results, I implemented a similar evening routine. Instead of checking the news, watching television, or going on social media, I looked inward. I wrote down three things I was grateful for and one goal I could accomplish the next day. The next morning, I would wake up and read my goals with the same sense of calm and focus that I had ended my day with.

What these new routines do is replace those rote habits that aren't serving us in any meaningful way with new ones that bring us closer to our goals and into alignment with our personal *why-how-what*.

BUILDING A WHY STACK FROM YOUR PERSONAL *WHY-HOW-WHAT*

In workshops, this exercise is done in conjunction with someone else. As this is a book for self-study, you might find it is tempting to read through the 9 WHYs and just pick the one *why* that most resonates with you. However, going through the process with someone else can be much more engaging and illuminating. Discovering your *why* brings that aha moment best shared with someone whom you can work with—a person who can ask you clarifying questions to get to the bottom of your story and its meaning to you.

With that in mind, I recommend you begin by visiting whyinstitute.com and using their free app to help determine your *why*. Once you've received the result, you can choose to continue online or look closely at the other 9 WHYs and then work with a good friend to discover their personal *why-how-what* and build their Why Stack. Doing this will help you understand the process. Ideally, your friend can ask you the same questions in return. The goal is for each of you to articulate to the other why you do what you do and how you go about doing it to reach a place of mutual understanding, thereby creating a stronger connection.

If you don't have access to the app, the next best first step would be to help someone else connect with their *why* first. In this case, you share only a quick overview with them, as many will try to guess the outcome without focusing on the process, and the process is the entire point of this exercise.

To start, ask your partner in this effort to share their story of a recent work-related interaction (ideally within the last three months) that they came away from feeling good about three things: themselves, the other person, and the interaction itself. The interaction that they share should be work related and person to person, either by phone or face-to-face. An email or text-message interaction doesn't work, and neither does a negative interaction. Be sure to ask several more open-ended questions that aren't answerable by a simple yes or no. Keep the dialogue going, listen for keywords, and pay attention to their facial expressions. Note what they were saying when they made that broad smile, as they are making that connection to their *why*.

After the first story, ask the partner to share another story of an interaction, this time outside of work, where the partner came away with the same feeling—good about themselves, the other person, and the interaction.

Some people need to tell two or three stories to get to their *why*. Without interrupting, you can ask questions that connect the partner to their feelings via their limbic brain, as opposed to via their neocortex, or their logical brain. This isn't about your connecting the partner to their *why*. It's about helping them make the connection themselves. There are no right or wrong answers, and there is no judgment. Remember, it's their story based on their experience, through their lens on life.

For instance, if in each story the person mentions *trust*, it's a good idea to follow with "Tell me a little bit more about what trust means to you." Reflecting on what you hear and asking for clarification allows you to become an active listener to their stories and the stories of others. It takes a lot of time and practice to be able to listen to understand and accept, as we are so used to listening in order to give our opinions.

When it seems clear what the *why* might be, go back to chapter two and hand it to your partner and ask them to read it. (This can also be done quickly by using the *why* app developed by Dr. Sanchez. Here's the link: http://whyinstitute.com.)

How do they feel when they read it? What does their body language or tone of voice suggest?

If someone feels stuck between two *whys*, ask another clarifying question. For example, a question for a person who is stuck between "contributing" or "finding a better way and sharing it," may go like this: "Does it feel better when you help someone directly or if you give them some ideas as to what is needed to help them do things?" Giving them a choice between two *whys*—in this case, "to contribute and "a better way"—allows them to choose which one resonates with them at a more personal level. Get them to feel versus think.

Once you have the *why* in place, identify the *what*. Even though the order is *why-how-what*, the *how* acts as a bridge between the first two, I found it easier to uncover what the outcome (what I do) was and then go back to link my *why* and *what* through *how* I do things.

To identify the *what*, say, "Share with me what makes you feel good when you have accomplished something." If there are a number of answers, narrow the options down by asking, "Of the following three possibilities, is it that you challenged the status quo, helped make sense of the complicated, or contributed to the end result?" This should help to identify that person's *what*. Our *what* is the impact that we have on the world around us. It's how we touch the lives of others.

The bridge between the two (*why* and *what*) is our *how*. Our *how* is derived from our skills, talents, strengths, and determination, among other things. It's through our *how* that we effectively express ourselves. It's our *how* that makes each of us unique in the world. It's also what CliftonStrengths bases a large part of their work on. Our *how* is where our talents and strengths reside and is the means with which we best express ourselves, creatively, physically, and verbally. Our talents only become actual strengths when we invest our time, energy, and resources to realize our potential.

When our *why*, *how*, and *what* are in alignment, we are often living at our best. Whether personally or professionally, when these three come together, it's an optimal feeling. Imagine living at 100 percent, navigating from the simple to the most complex of tasks!

IDENTIFYING YOUR WHY STACK

Once you have helped someone identify and build their Why Stack, hand this book to them and ask them to walk you through the same process. Now that they've connected with and shaped their Why Stack, you can start the process to build and connect with yours.

These Why Stack exercises can be all-consuming, so take a break, let all you have learned settle in, and then start your journey of discovery.

CHAPTER FIVE

THE LUNGE

The lunge was developed in fencing to instantly bridge the distance gap between the attacking fencer and the opponent. The goal in the attacker's mind, as always, is to score a touch, and a well-executed lunge is the quickest way to close the distance separating the two fencers. The perfect lunge is a release of energy at the right time, attaining the right distance for scoring. The lunge is similar to our *how*, in that when we fully engage, everything comes together for that one moment, and we feel fully in tune with our surroundings as we move away from our comfort zone into new territory.

In life, students work toward their degrees, athletes reach for championships, musicians prepare for concerts, and entrepreneurs work toward changing their communities through running a successful enterprise. Each of us attempts to bridge the gap between our current state of being and our desired state of doing.

To start, we have to push both our physical and mental selves to new limits on an incremental basis. We need to exercise, to stretch our bodies and our brains to consider new possibilities. Where and who do we want to be in ninety days? In six months? In a year? Our minds need to bridge that gap.

Good footwork in fencing means taking one or two quick steps back, then four slower steps forward, then another couple of steps back, and a few more forward. This constant movement is what sets up the lunge because just standing there thinking about what your next move should be creates zero momentum! Fencers need to disguise their intent, which good footwork can do when setting up the lunge so that the opponent won't have time to respond.

However, footwork on its own, without a precise calculation needed to cover the distance and achieve the end goal of a touch, is a waste of energy. Movement without purpose doesn't lead to success, just as developing a plan without executing it isn't going to change anything. When we know *what* we want to do and *why* we want to do it, we need to bridge this with *how* we're going to do it. Our *how* is the way we execute. The connection between our *why* and our *how* is very "*me*"-centric, and we only become successful when the connection between our *how* and *what* connects us with others to become more "*we*"-centric. The diagram below will help visualize what I mean here:

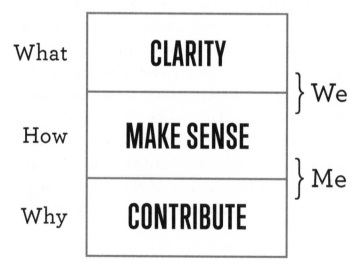

As Simon Sinek mentions, people don't simply connect with *what* you do; they connect with *how* you got there and then with *why* you did it. Scoring a goal or point is important. What is more important for future learning is *how* it was done. The same applies to success in businesses. If a company reaches a target using unethical practices, people will not focus on the goal that was met. Instead, they will focus on the questionable tactics the company or individual took to get there. Just look at all the recent dishonor in professional sports and the overflow of case studies where businesses put profits before people. The *how* clearly matters!

I met a woman on a flight to California who moved to Los Angeles to become an actress. It was a long flight, and apart from the polite "I see you're sitting next to me" smile, we hadn't spoken a word for the first several hours. With one hour left, we started chatting, and she mentioned her big move and career change. When I asked her why she wanted to be an actress, she didn't have a clear answer beyond the standard "It's something I've always wanted to do," so I offered to help her connect with her *why*. She discovered that hers was to *simplify*. I was expecting the usual aha moment, yet somehow, the discovery that her *why* was to simplify didn't seem unique to her.

"Well, doesn't everyone do it this way?" she asked. To her, it was natural to simplify complex human emotions into a role that audiences could identify with. I then asked her how she did what she did, and she came to realize that by doing things the right way, she simplified things. Only then did she have her aha moment. She finally understood why she wanted to be an actress: to simplify human emotions into roles people resonated with and were moved by.

If she could do things the right way to simplify roles for people, then she would thrive in that profession by creating clarity for her audience.

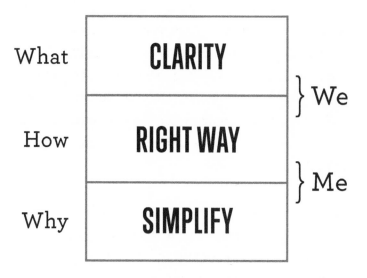

Knowing your personal *why-how-what* in a workplace setting is critical to long-term career success. When teammates know their own Why Stack, they can better articulate the reason behind the methods they use. When coming from a position of authenticity, articulating goals and how you will attain them creates clarity. Teams who know each other's Why Stack can more easily acknowledge and play to their individual and team strengths instead of focusing on weaknesses.

When we are aligned with our Why Stack, people around us take notice. We demonstrate more energy through our actions and thereby build more capacity to succeed. It doesn't happen overnight. Small shifts eventually lead to results that others notice. Someone who goes to the gym every night after work and changes their diet to lose weight will eventually start to hear from people who see their progress. A writer who wakes up at five in the morning to write for an extra hour each day will eventually create a book people can hold and read. Family members and colleagues take notice when someone is operating at a higher capacity because it inspires and impacts them as well.

The best companies hire people with a broader range of Why Stacks. If everyone fell in the same category, such as "simplify" or "the right way," then the organization would have limited resources in terms of employees who could offer many different ways to approach overcoming whatever challenges the organization may have to meet. Diversity of thought is really important within teams and companies. When everyone represents a different *why* and can express this through their individual *how*, their impact expands exponentially because they are part of a well-rounded team.

Daniel James Brown writes about the rowing crew of the University of Washington and how they competed in the 1936 Berlin Olympics when the Germans were favored to win. *The Boys in the Boat* serves as a useful analogy for the importance of variety and inclusion within a team, bringing together the "overtly aggressive oarsmen" likely to wipe themselves out in the first stages of the race and the "strong introverts" less likely to be overwhelmed by the competitiveness within:

> Good crews are good blends of personalities: someone to lead the charge, someone to hold something in reserve; someone to pick a fight, someone to make peace; someone to think things through, someone to charge ahead without thinking. Somehow all this must mesh. That's the steepest challenge...Even after the right mixture is found, each man or woman in the boat must recognize his or her place in the fabric of the crew, accept it, and accept the others as they are. It is an exquisite thing when it all comes together in just the right way. The intense bonding and the sense of exhilaration that results from it are what many oarsmen row for, far more than for trophies or accolades.

Wherever you are, in a boat or in a business, you need to trust those ahead of you and behind you. When everyone is doing their share, it becomes important to respect and understand the value of the contribution that each person makes.

The wider the gap between the work that you do and your Why Stack, the greater the discord. We walk down paths that take us further away from our goal and purpose. Negativity sets in, and we expend more energy on doing things we shouldn't have to do, leaving less energy for the things we wish we could do. When we combat dissonance with resonance and operate from a place of flow and clarity, what we're doing reaffirms our reason for doing it.

A few years ago, with my three siblings, we took a trip to Fox Glacier in New Zealand to celebrate a milestone birthday. It was the first time in our lives that just the four of us had been together as adults, and none of us had ever done anything like this trek before. We rented all the necessary equipment for the adventure and set off into unfamiliar terrain. We trekked over dry riverbeds, trudged through humid tropical forests, and stumbled up a frozen icy-blue glacier.

Along the way, we poked at what looked like stable ground to make sure it was safe and stopped to put on layers as the temperatures dropped. It was a long, slow process. A big part of the reason that the trek took so long was that we didn't know what to expect or how to navigate the unforeseen challenges ahead. In other words, the path ahead was unclear.

On the other hand, our guide was confident and agile, pickax at the ready. He moved quickly from one side to the other, always moving forward while the rest of us looked at our feet, concerned about where to place our next step. His knowledge of the terrain and his experience as a qualified guide gave him confidence in his responsibility (to bring us home safely) and gave him the clarity on how to choose the best route to make our experience safe and memorable.

We made it to our goal, drank some well-earned, clear, ice-cold water right off the glacier, took a few family pictures, felt like we had conquered our own mini Everest, and set our sights on the way back.

Somehow, the return journey seemed shorter, even though we went back pretty much the same way and at a similar pace. Time flew by, as we were now a bit more familiar with our surroundings. Although we still had to pay attention to the terrain, we were now fully appreciative of the beautiful panorama that stretched out below us. We had clarity, which allowed us to move quickly and with confidence and to see things we didn't see on the way up. All the while, our guide smiled as we took in more and more of the moment. Similar to our guide, we are all experts in some areas of our lives and can easily lead others within our areas of expertise. Once we know our personal *why-how-what*, we can be clearer on where we're going and help show others the way.

Everyone has the ability to be a mentor in someone else's life. What might be missing is the opportunity to become one, because when we are not aware of why we do what we do, we don't even think about how we could be a mentor. Once we have this greater awareness, we are presented with an opportunity to reach out and guide someone else.

BE A GUIDE

We are all guides when we use our perspective and experience to show someone how to accomplish things. We may show and/or teach someone to do something as simple as tying a shoe or as creative as designing a shoe. In guiding others, we help them close the gap between where they are and where they want to be.

- Who can you be a guide for?

- How can you help show the way for them to start their journey?

CHAPTER SIX

THE FLÈCHE

Flèche is French for "arrow," and in fencing, it's a move where a fencer strikes, catching the opponent by surprise. It's the fullest extension of the body and can carry one further than a lunge. As with many aspects of fencing, the most important element of a flèche is the timing that creates the surprise for the opponent.

For six years in a row, I competed and placed in the USA Fencing National Championships in the 50–59 category. The 50–59 category competes to ten touches, and over the years, I placed as high as second place (twice) and third place (twice) and as far back as ninth and seventeenth... never first!

In the final match of the 2015 championships, after a long day that played out over six hours of fencing and waiting, I had a 4–2 lead in the gold medal bout. I felt like I blinked for a few moments there and was suddenly trailing at 4–6. (Clearly, I had lost focus and was stuck in thinking what my next move would be instead of actually doing it.) Quickly, I refocused and tied it at six all. My opponent scored the next touch and led 7–6. With ten seconds remaining before the one-minute break, I decided to give it my all and attack him. Before I could, he stepped back, opened the distance between us, parried, and hit me with his riposte. The score was 6–8 at halftime.

At the one-minute break, my coach asked, "What were you thinking with that move and with only ten seconds left on the clock?"

I said that I "thought" it was the right moment. He reminded me that I needed to focus and truly "feel" that right moment, as there was little margin for error, given the tight score. My opponent needed only two touches to win, and I needed two to tie and two more to win. This guy was a solid, strong fencer over six feet tall, while I'm barely five foot six in my fencing shoes. It was now ten in the evening, and the long day of fencing matches and beating all our other opponents along the way was catching up with us.

After the break, I noticed my opponent was agitated, while I felt calm and focused. I tied the score at 8-8. As I slowly set up my next move and launched my attack, he quickly ended that moment with another good parry, then a solid riposte, and led 9-8. I was determined not to lose and scored the next touch on my go-for-broke flèche that landed on target. We were now tied 9-9.

I knew this was it, and "the moment" was going to happen for one of us. As we got back on guard, I planned for another flèche attack to win the match. I remembered that he was stronger and his fencing style more aggressive. I believed I was faster and had better footwork. As all these thoughts and hypothetical situations were starting to play in my head, suddenly reality took hold fast. He initiated his big attack, and I instinctively took a small step back and then a half step forward. It was these two simple steps that allowed me to quickly close the distance. While my flèche never materialized, his went right by me. The timing and distance were perfect for that one moment. I scored and finally won that elusive championship 10-9.

I had been fencing for decades before that championship match. It was only five years before that match that I had decided to rededicate myself to training with a specific purpose in mind. Because I executed my plan throughout the day, I did the work to win the championship and pushed myself to arrive at the crucial moment that would give me the opportunity to win. When it came down to the wire, a split-second decision determined the end result of all my training.

The Why Stack is like an archer's bow, arrow, and target. When we visualize what we have to do, we know when to release the arrow to go to where it needs to go. If we lack confidence, we miss the target. If we don't know why we do what we do, we won't know how to hit that bull's-eye. It goes without saying that—as in fencing—a moving target is much harder to hit if you don't anticipate where the target might be going.

As a competitor and sports enthusiast, I have learned a lot from Olympians, their coaches, and my instructors, often seeking their counsel and advice after a tough loss. They universally shared the belief that identifying the right time for the right action is not only difficult, it's also a fleeting moment that must be seized. While many external elements must come together to set up the opportune moment, it is up to us to create a perfect moment within that exact space in time in order to experience success. When we have a plan and are in alignment, the timing that is required becomes much clearer. Over the years, I've learned that routine statements such as

New Year's resolutions often fall flat because they are thoughts without a plan. There's no clarity around when to start, what it really takes, or how to get to that desired point and beyond.

At a certain point in our commitment to change, we get close enough to our goal to intentionally release that last bit of energy needed to take us over the final hurdle. Unfortunately, there can be times when our inner critic holds us back from fully letting us go where we really want to go.

With every new undertaking in life, we start off motivated and initially emotionally engaged. We run seven days in a row or sign up for every guitar lesson we can cram into our schedule. Then on the eighth day of running, our feet hurt, or after the tenth guitar lesson, our fingers hurt, and we decide to take it easy and back off. As we lose that initial drive, the inner critic creeps in, and in due time, it takes over.

Our inner critic, no matter how or why we came to have one, thrives on our fears and impedes progress. Our inner critic doesn't lead. Instead, it causes us to recede. It constantly negotiates with us to do less, try less, risk less. Our inner critic is blocked and lost. Instead of listening, it reacts—often angrily. Our inner critic distracts us from our purpose.

What we need to do to diminish the power of the inner critic is to choose to cultivate the mindset of a warrior. The warrior mindset becomes our inner leader who operates from a place of flow. The warrior guides with focus, determination, clarity, and purpose.

Operating within a warrior mindset allows us to stick to the path that we wish to follow. When we start out on the journey to where we want to be, we need a clear path. If we don't have a plan, if we take the goat trails that appear as shortcuts along the way, distracted, we will zigzag across the terrain, taking a lot longer to get to our destination, trying one road and then another. When we know our personal *why-how-what*, it's clear where we're supposed to go and what it will take to get there. Even though there will be unforeseen speed bumps and obstacles, the warrior mindset will carry us through.

As the critical mind is what holds us back, the warrior mindset is an inner fighting spirit that's clear on *why* we need to forge ahead. How we go about addressing a specific challenge makes a difference in whether or not we'll succeed.

Losing a match, not getting a job, or stumbling at a particular task doesn't have to be a huge setback. It can be disappointing, and dealing with that disappointment gives us a basis to pause, reflect, and learn from the experience. By keeping the warrior mindset front and center, we can plan the steps needed to try again and again with determination.

What's your mindset like when you feel challenged? How about when a task feels insurmountable?

NINETY-DAY PLAN

- Identify your personal *why-how-what*.

- What do you want to accomplish?

- What are the rituals you need to integrate into your daily life?

- What do you have to start doing to succeed?

- What do you have to stop doing to succeed?

- What will you do less of?

- What will you do more of?

- What does success mean and look like for you?

- What will you commit to doing over the next ninety days to attain your goal?

Breaking things down into manageable chunks makes goals easier to attain. Action items become less daunting, and the inner critic won't creep in as easily. Instead, the warrior says, "It's only three months. What's the big deal?"

To succeed, track progress using an online or off-line tool or app that works best with your way of learning. By holding yourself accountable, measuring your progress, and adjusting the tempo along the way, you can stay on your chosen path.

In fencing, when you know your plan, you are prepared and can easily spot that moment of opportunity when it presents itself. Without a plan, you can't. To make it happen, work and live your plan.

CHAPTER SEVEN

GETTING BACK ON GUARD

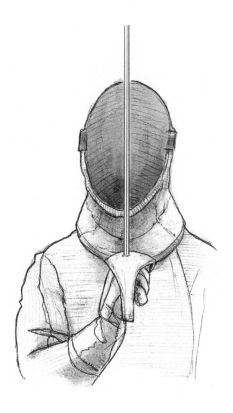

In a bout, regardless of whether you score a touch or your opponent scores one against you, both fencers have to immediately get back on guard to be ready for the next encounter. After scoring a touch, one fencer will briefly celebrate that touch, either internally or externally, while the other fencer thinks about what they need to do next. In life, when we reach a milestone or accomplish a goal, it's important to celebrate the moment and prepare for the next stage that's coming shortly thereafter. No matter what happens, we have to get back on guard. At the end of a tough day at work, for example, we go home, shift tempo to become fully present for our loved ones and then, make the time to prepare for what might be in store for us the following day. When we know we have to get back on guard, how do we best prepare for what's next?

Getting back on guard is more than being physically present. It's being mentally and emotionally present as well, regardless of what just happened. If you have to be at work at nine in the morning, do you start to get ready when you walk in, or are you ready before you enter the office? When you sit down (or stand) at your desk, are you ready to tackle your tasks, or do you need fifteen minutes to warm up? Being ready for your day is just as important as being ready before you fence.

In movies, there's often a dramatic moment when two people look at each other and ask, "Ready?" and then go do whatever they built up to do in that dramatic moment. Whether they jump off a cliff, attack aliens, or head out on a great adventure, they have to be ready for it so that we can follow them on their journey in the story that's playing out in front of us.

When I chose to write a blog every week for a year, I had to reset each time I posted a new one and come up with something original for the following week. Little did I know that a few years later, this would help me with writing a book for the first time.

In fencing, the pressure to be ready is constant. If you compete in ten or twelve bouts in a day, you may have only short breaks between matches. How do you cultivate the mental energy to keep going if you're running on empty? How do you handle mental and physical fatigue? Regardless of what happened a second ago, fencers need to hit the reset button and focus on what's immediately in front of them.

At times, I've been so angry with myself after a match that I packed up and left, arriving so early at the airport that I would spend hours on my own, replaying the moments that got away from me in my head. At other times, with a more balanced perspective, I realized that by staying and watching from the stands, I could learn more about how an opponent actually beat me by observing their next match. In one instance, a fencer who beat me quickly lost to the next opponent—someone I had beaten several times in the past. This showed me that you never know which version of yourself will show up on the fencing strip on any given day.

If a fencer loses early in the day and is eliminated from a tournament, there are two choices to make: pack up your bag, close your mind, and go home, or stay, watch the people who win, and learn from their success. Win or lose, once you get home, you have to do the laundry.

The night I won the national championship, I returned to my brother's house with a bag of sweaty and rather pungent fencing gear. After that long day of competing, those sporting clothes were at their worst. I had to take everything out, wash it, and hang it out to dry. There was no way those things could be put in my fencing bag for the return trip! I didn't have a place to hang the clothes, so I used a foosball table on a nearby patio. I hung my national championship medal beside all my equipment that made for one successful day and took a picture, as a reminder that even as a champion, you still have to go home and do the laundry in order to start your next day with a clean slate.

If you lose a bid or a client in business, do you stay and ask questions to gain a greater understanding of why or how this happened, or do you dismiss it as a loss and move on to something else?

It takes discipline to stay and learn. Overcoming the emotions that swirl around a loss is the first step. Setting them aside, as a next step, allows us to think about what to do better next time in order to reach our goal. Sometimes the disappointment can feel so great that you can't bring yourself to stay in the room, let alone get back on track. By asking for clarification or watching an outcome unfold in front of you, you can better determine what is needed when a similar scenario starts to replay for you in the future. You can visualize what you have to change and how.

Whenever you might lose, you don't have to start from square one. You have the foundation of what you have already learned—that's how you came to be in a position to compete in the first place. To get to the next level, you'll go through similar preparatory stages more fluidly than the previous times because you're drawing from what you've learned along the way and are no longer in the same place as when you started. A loss or a rejection isn't the end of anything. It's an opportunity to learn and move up.

You can choose to learn from that loss, move on, and grow, or relive that loss and remain small, which is not likely to give you much insight into how to change. The inner critic relives a loss. The inner critic mulls it over and replays it in its mind, while the warrior chooses to learn from the loss. The warrior asks, "Where am I now as a result of that loss? What is my next positive step as a result of that loss?"

During the quarterfinals at the Rio Olympics, a US fencer was down 8–14 against an Italian opponent. Being only one touch away from that decisive fifteenth touch, (in the open divisions, fencers compete to 15 touches in 3 periods vs. 10 touches in 2 periods for the veteran age groups) the Italian fencer felt very confident about his chances of winning. He was psyching himself up after scoring the fourteenth touch and confidently wagged his "number one" index finger, knowing that one point was all it would take to end the match. Yet the American came back on the next touch and the next one and the next one. He was seemingly unstoppable, tying up the score at 14–14.

It's extremely difficult to come back and score seven touches in a row, especially when the opponent needs only one touch to win. At 14–14, they both got back on guard and were ready. The fans went from shouting loudly in support of their favorite to holding their collective breath in silence. Both fencers knew this was it: that one moment in time that they had trained for most of their lives. At the crucial moment of an intense back-and-forth, the American executed a solid fencing action and won 15-14. He had made it to the top four and was on his way to an Olympic medal in the finals!

The Italian's mindset was "I need one more touch."

The American's mindset was "I need the next touch."

While these two may sound similar, they are worlds apart. The Italian got caught up thinking he needed only one more touch to win, while the American was focused uniquely on the *next* touch. What's the difference? It's the distinction between focusing on the result (winning) and focusing on the process (scoring the next touch). While one fencer focused on the result, the need for one more to finish, the other fencer focused on the process. Even though the American had further to go from where he was, he got there before his opponent.

I wonder what the American learned from being down and coming back for a win and what the Italian learned from losing when he had only one touch to go? Sports are so interesting as analogies to life because they present many opportunities to reset, learn, and continue upward. For me, the core question remains "How hard are you willing to work to get to that next level?"

The American clearly embodied the warrior mindset on that day, resetting after each touch. With each new "on guard," he dug a little bit deeper into his mental and physical capacity to access the energy needed to stay in the game and continue.

That's the whole point: to continue to advance upward. Winning a local event leads to a regional event, winning the regional leads to a national event, and winning that leads to a world championship and the ultimate venue for minor sports, the Olympic Games. Each step leads to something else. The ability to reset, and refocus at specific moments, is what leads to success.

Getting back on guard is akin to getting in alignment with your Why Stack. In doing so, you build up a set of skills that become more and more refined over time, turning them into strengths that you can count on. Getting back on guard is not easy. If you face a daunting task or a life-changing challenge look inward to your strengths to compliment any outside support you may need. While going through the CliftonStrengths certification process, I learned about the importance of understanding how we live and thrive through accessing our strengths. And, similar to the connection I made between the 9 whys and our personal *why, how, what*, I realized there was a strong link between the *how* of the Why Stack and the top 5 CliftonStrengths: Here's what I learned about myself:

How I make sense of complex situations draws largely

from my strong feeling of *Belief* in the link between that past and the future (*Context*) that allows me to manage my time and energy to help others improve (*Developer*). Additionally, I will use my resilience in the face of perceived failure (*Positivity*) to create genuine and mutually rewarding relationships that last over time (*Relator*). Once I'm able to make sense of things through the filter of my strengths, then I'm better able to create clarity for others, which is what I enjoy doing the most.

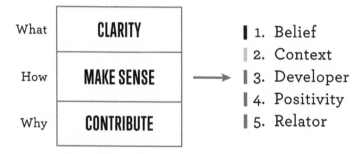

To learn more about CliftonStrengths take their top 5 or full 34 assessment here: https://www.gallupstrengthscenter.com. Then line your strengths up next to the *how* of your Why Stack to gain even more insight into your strengths and how you express yourself in your own a unique way.

In life, we need to come back to our personal *why-how-what* to recharge and recenter using our strengths. As long as we stick to working our plan, we can climb back into the moment and re-create the flow, and in doing so, we can rise to the occasion.

- Write down a time you lost—a game, a tournament, a client, an opportunity.

- What did you learn?

- What were you willing to do to get back in and try again?

- How did you turn this into a win?

Years ago, I cofounded Hyperwerks, an independent comic book company. One of the books we set out to publish was based on a Persian mythical hero called Rostam, whose story was written down well over one thousand years ago by the Persian poet Ferdowsi. On Rostam's journey through life, he battles both inner and outer demons, much like the modern-day character of Batman.

At certain points, his greatest nemesis is himself. He has to fight the darkness inside him.

Interestingly enough, the character we know as Batman has continued to evolve over time. Few people realize that when Batman made it onto television in the 1960s, the character had been diverted away from the darker moods of the original comic book series. He and his sidekick, Robin, were portrayed with exaggerated and campy "Bang! Pow! Whap!" moves and noises. It was cartoonish and cheesy, and for some fans, Batman had lost its essence. Michael Uslan was fourteen when the TV series aired, and as a huge fan of the original Batman comics, he was crushed to see this portrayal of a character he loved.

When Michael Uslan "grew up," he became the world's first professor to teach about comics, and he went on to write for DC Comics. For a while, it seemed as if Batman had all but disappeared from the cultural consciousness, and Uslan decided to buy certain Batman rights when DC had all but given up on the Dark Knight. Now, he's known for producing high-grossing Batman films that have been eagerly received by a global fan base for decades. He changed the perception of Batman.

On a smaller scale, we wanted to give Rostam's story, one that had survived over a millennium, a new life, and make it relevant for a broader readership base. Traditionalists objected to our adaptation and continued to loudly challenge our interpretation even after we had won an international award (Golden Lioness) that took us to Budapest. What started as a cool idea to reframe a valuable story largely unknown to the Western world took on a life of its own.

When you have a vision, and you're determined to accomplish it, the journey will unfold in a way you may never expect. The young Michael Uslan was on a mission to save Batman, and in turn, he impacted the lives of thousands of artists and actors and millions of fans.

To bring it back to the Why Stack, the reason I embarked on that journey with the Rostam story was in part to contribute in a small way to my cultural background. I wanted to be a part of something bigger than myself and create clarity for an audience who hadn't heard the story. We did this by working closely with our team to make sense of the complicated storylines deeply rooted in tradition. At the time, I had no idea this project aligned fully with my Why Stack.

ALIGNING YOUR ACCOMPLISHMENTS

Look back on your accomplishments. How do they align with your Why Stack? Where are the common threads, and what do these mean to you now? Or if something went awry, what aspect of why something went off track is now clear to you?

We often embark on projects or go down paths without necessarily knowing why. Instead of over-focusing on the bad habits we repeatedly engage in, take some time to reflect on the positive things that have happened and connect them to your personal *why-how-what*.

For instance,

- Why did you study one subject and not another?

- How did it feel playing to your strengths as opposed to trying to prop up your weaknesses?

- What have you gained from this knowledge, and how are you using it in life?

The inner critic takes up a lot of our mental bandwidth and energy. The warrior needs to be front and center instead.

CHAPTER EIGHT

MOVING UP

When we work toward a goal, the peak of the mountain where we've placed that goal often feels very far away. There's a different kind of mindset needed to move upward. It's easier to dream than to take those vital first steps to ascend. In fencing, the need to move up the bracket is clear: the only way to the top is through someone else. Sometimes, though, our greatest opponent is our other self. We lose because we get in our own way. Too often we are the greatest hindrance to our own success.

In mountaineering, it's one step at a time to the summit. You need the right guide, the right gear, and the right team. When you reach the peak, you're only halfway—you need to come back down. Along the way up, you first need to align with your team, then accelerate awareness, and then focus as you reach a certain level. Once there, you can acclimate before starting again on your upward climb.

In life, you need to do the same—align, accelerate, acclimate. At times, you push yourself harder to access your next level and create stepping stones along your path to revisit when times get tough.

When people reach a summit too quickly and then crash and burn, it's often because they didn't take the time to acclimate. They most likely worked very hard to get to the top; however, once they had "arrived," they were not able to stay there. If we're not in alignment, important foundations can fall apart. We risk a rapid deceleration and can spiral off in another direction, one we never saw coming.

This deceleration happens when we're unable to operate consistently and with intensity at a high level. Great athletes, artists, leaders, and entrepreneurs can accelerate when needed and have the awareness to acclimate each time they reach a higher level. Someone who rockets to the top without learning what it takes to stay there can come to a grinding halt and is not at the top for very long before experiencing a quick descent.

Imagine competing in a fencing tournament on a Sunday and winning, qualifying for the national championships, coming down off that natural high, and hours later, you're flying or driving back home. On Monday, you wake up early, feeling stiffness in your legs, lower back, upper body, even your neck, yet you head to the gym regardless, committing to the same routine you had before you won that tournament. What keeps you going? After a match or a milestone, the process has to start all over again. We go back to training, taking another lesson, reestablishing footwork and fundamentals at a higher level. The goal of all of this continued activity is to keep moving upward.

When we reach a certain level, there is an inflection point and a choice. Do I stay here, get acclimated, and remain comfortable? Or do I start the process again in order to ascend even higher this time around?

This could be a new goal or another tier of the same goal. When we are clear in our intent, our goals appear more reasonable and more urgent. At each stage in the process of accomplishment, we hit an inflection point—the place where we need to decide how to proceed. During the entire length of this journey, we are constantly acclimating, aligning, and accelerating in order to ascend to the next level.

This is how businesses move from the kitchen table to the garage to a coworking space and, finally, to their own building. Entrepreneurs often grow their businesses in this way, be it slowly and organically with their own money, or rapidly and in partnership with other people's money. You have to scale up and build your enterprise one stage at a time. How fast you get there is based on your capacity to excel and accelerate, all the while knowing 100 percent why you're doing it in the first place.

Your ability to acclimate when you reach a new plateau is necessary, much as it is necessary for experienced climbers to take their time to acclimate to new altitudes before they take the next crucial step. Competitors need to adjust at each stage to reenergize themselves for the next set of challenges. When you push yourself, you increase your capacity to change your attitude toward what you once believed was not attainable.

Aligning is the equivalent of getting back on guard. We all need to check in with our Why Stack and ready ourselves for what's next. Do we have what we need to succeed at this new level—the equipment, a plan, a support system? We need to take this moment to align everything before we accelerate and ascend.

Once everything is in the right place, we can move toward where we want to go. Use your Why Stack as a filter to measure your decision making.

Acceleration is the result of the right discipline and the right motivation coming together to maintain a higher pace. When you train, for instance, you want to always finish on a high note. Good coaches won't let you stop working at it until you get the move right because ending a session with that accomplishment is what enables the athlete to stay engaged until the next practice. We all need discipline to try and try and try until the goal is reached. That discipline supports your motivation because the effort required to finish the job on a high note instills confidence. You're more likely to come back and practice when you're confident both as to why you practice so hard and to how you're going to get better each time.

Again, motivation is what gets us to the starting line, while determination helps us cross the finish line. Picture thirty thousand highly motivated and energized runners at the start of a marathon. Less than half are determined to cross the finish line in under four hours. Even for those who are determined to do so, motivation is hard to keep up when you reach that twenty-three-mile mark, and your body looks at you from the inside and says, "Are you kidding me?" Those last 3.2 miles are when your determination needs to kick in. It's what keeps you going. It's the result of the discipline needed during the hours spent on training to conquer the blisters, the headaches, and all those sore muscles. Doing all that's needed during those long days, weeks, and months that blend into years to overcome a challenge or meet a goal comes from a determined mindset. There's little that can stop a person who knows their purpose and is determined to see it through.

For example, a writer would start by writing in a journal each day, perhaps advance to writing a blog, and finally move to working on a manuscript for a book. Each of these steps takes a person's skills to the next level.

Once we ascend to a new level, we go right back to the start of the process, acclimating all over again. All of this is helping us get closer to our purpose, which is defined via our Why Stack.

RECOGNIZE YOUR LEVEL

Some people are content with participating at a local or recreational level. That's their capacity for that particular undertaking and where they feel happy. A different group will keep pushing themselves to higher levels, where the air is thinner. High performers thrive when they operate at the highest level in many aspects of their lives.

When we know our *why*, our goals become more reasonable, purposeful, and urgent.

CHAPTER NINE

FINAL TOUCH

There's a subtle difference between the last touch and the final touch in fencing. The last touch is one in a series of touches that leads a fencer to win a bout. The final touch is the one that ends the match. When you score the final touch, it's over. There's a great sense of relief and release of tension in having won. In fencing tournaments, winning athletes will shout with intensity and either jump as high as they can or fall to their knees. Although they're mentally calm beforehand, they often lose it in the moment of celebration because all their concentration and hard work comes down to that moment when expectations were met and dreams were realized.

In life, we need to prepare for the final touch—the moment when all our preparation and concentration comes together for success. We see it with athletes in the arena of competition, with musicians playing a concert, with artists at a gallery opening. These are special moments that really matter, whether it's a standing ovation, an award, or a congratulatory expression from a complete stranger who recognizes their work. It's the moment when everything comes together.

When you can envision what that final touch looks and feels like—and know why you're going for it—then you must move toward your goal with intent.

What are you willing to give up to accomplish your goals?

What bad habits will you need to let go of in order to succeed? What will you say *no* to now in order to say *yes* to future accomplishments?

The alternative approach is to keep asking, "Why am I doing this?" That is, "Why am I doing the same thing over and over and getting the same results?" How do you break the cycle? How do you jump off that hamster wheel that rolls around and around going nowhere? If you're happy on the hamster wheel, that's fine. Stay there. If you feel unfulfilled, then figure out a way to challenge your status quo to change that feeling and uncovering a better way. Knowing your personal *why-how-what* makes giving up on the wheel and entering into a different phase of your life—a more integrated life—a powerful starting point. There's nothing more depressing than watching that wheel spin around while the hamster inside that spinning wheel is lifeless.

Tony Robbins said, "Change happens when the pain of staying the same is greater than the pain of change." Anaïs Nin said, "And the day came when the risk to remain tight in a bud was more painful than the risk it took to blossom."

All of us possess a certain tolerance for the pain caused by not changing. Lowering that level of tolerance is key to taking action, and working toward change gives us a true feeling of freedom.

Many people remark that they need to lose weight or that they need to stop smoking. There are countless things we know we *need* to do—or not do—until we truly *want* to, we won't make the commitment to continued action. When we truly want something, we imbue it with meaning. Our wants are what drive us.

Once we actually start writing, training, or practicing, we want to do it more and more. The emotions around doing something that we were initially uncomfortable with will change, and what used to hold us back fades as we gain traction and start to firmly believe in ourselves just that much more day after day. When you work hard to establish a rhythm, you will accomplish certain goals faster when they align with your well-defined purpose. It's simple. Take a *need to do*, turn it into a *want to do*, and convert that into *doing*.

Knowing your *why* takes away excuses. When you know your reason for doing something, you can't ask, "Why am I doing this?" You have the answer. You know exactly why. What's important is to pursue the action based on the answer. Excuses hold us all back, as much as answers push us all forward. There are no longer excuses when we know our *why-how-what*.

Now that you have the knowledge, what are you going to do with it?

Acting on your knowledge turns it into an experience, and over time, experience becomes wisdom and expertise to share with others.

After you celebrate the final touch, you move on to that coveted top spot on the podium. That moment at the top is to be celebrated, shared, and fully taken in. The next step up is to use this moment as a platform to what's next in your life—the next milestone, the next goal, the next stage. The results are a testament to your ability to commit to hard work, drive, and discipline. They are an accumulation of all your preparation and concentration— the often-used expression "blood, sweat, and tears"—that need to be recognized and channeled into that next step.

You return home after an accomplishment, go to sleep, and wake up the next day with a smile on your face and a bit more "pep in your step" as the old saying goes. How can you best use the lessons learned to recapture this feeling to keep advancing and moving upward?

Ideally, you now know how to think about why you do what you do, how you did it, and what you will do next. You'll think about transition, transformation, and change in some way, shape, or form. You'll gain another level of clarity that will lead to new confidence, courage, and action to take further steps in the direction that's right for you.

Having read this book, you will either act on what you have learned or close the book and put it on a shelf. The choice is yours.

When the final touch is scored, I'm exhausted and drained. I shake hands with my opponent first, then the referees and coaches. If I won, I would celebrate. If I lost, I would go back to the mental drawing board. Regardless of the result, I always returned to the fencing club to start my warm-ups with that essential basic footwork.

We often overcomplicate things, which leads to ambiguity about where to go next and what to do about it. By identifying and building our Why Stack, we gain the awareness needed to continue with clarity. We can make better sense of what to do, how to do it, and how to get back into position. Instead of overthinking, we need to start focusing on why certain actions make us feel good and why others don't, in other words, listen to and play to our strengths in life. This will help us get refocused. Otherwise, we continue to get in our own way and never reach that elusive final touch.

The final touch is ultimately up to you. The final spot on the podium is there. You just need to create opportunities to reach the top.

FINAL THOUGHTS

- Now that you have clarity, what are you going to do with it?

- How are you going to put this clarity to use on a daily basis?

- What opportunities are you creating for your life?

RECOMMENDED READING

Some of the books that have broadened my perspective over the years:

Coach Wooden and Me	Kareem Abdul-Jabbar
Conversational Intelligence	Judith Glaser
Conversations with Myself	Nelson Mandela
David and Goliath	Malcolm Gladwell
Decisive	Chip and Dan Heath
Drive	Daniel Pink
Eleven Rings	Phil Jackson
Essentialism	Greg McKeown
Good Leaders Ask Great Questions	John C. Maxwell
Man's Search for Meaning	Viktor Frankl
Mastery	George Leonard
Meditations	Marcus Aurelius
Obliquity	John Kay
Quiet Mind	David Kundtz
Sapiens	Yuval Noah Harari

Soar with Your Strengths	Donald O. Clifton
Start with Why	Simon Sinek
Tao of Jeet Kune Do	Bruce Lee
The Big Leap	Gay Hendricks
The Fighter's Mind	Sam Sheridan
The Little Prince	Antoine de Saint-Exupéry
The Power of Now	Eckhart Tolle
The Speed of Trust	Stephen M. R. Covey
The War of Art	Steven Pressfield
Understanding Michael Porter	Joan Magretta
Walking with the Wind	John Lewis

ACKNOWLEDGMENTS

Life is a team effort, and very little is accomplished without the right "teammates" to guide, teach, support, and encourage us along on our journey.

Thank you to my parents, Leora and Mehdy Douraghy, my siblings, Bejan, Cameron, and Camilla, for always, always being there unconditionally, through thick and thin. A personal extra "thank you" to our mother, for her diligent editing skills that helped make this book flow better.

Thanks to everyone in the fencing community, especially my longtime coaches Heizaburo Okawa and Misha Itkin. I have learned so much about mindset, focus, resetting, and recalibrating from both of you. And an extra salute to all the fencers and coaches at LAIFC who constantly challenge me to stay at the top of my game, from Saturday morning practices to competing at major tournaments.

To my mentor, Warren Rustand, to whom I owe a special sense of gratitude for showing me how to open doors to deeper learning and understanding that I didn't even know existed until we worked together.

Thanks to the amazing members of the Entrepreneur's Organization for sharing your experiences and being open to discovering your *whys* around the world and in different languages. You definitely helped me to build a better entrepreneur within me. Additional thanks to my E18 forum mates for continually checking in on updates and holding me accountable to finishing this book.

To Dr. Gary Sanchez for his passion, drive and determination to find a better way for the world to discover and articulate their *why*.

I also want to thank the team at Scribe, who worked closely with me on all the nuances and details to take this book from concept to print, to you, the reader.

Additional thanks to a great group of friends who I view as life and work teammates who put in their time, effort, and feedback to help make this book happen: The team at Artisan Creative, Dr. Christian Reichardt, Derek Cotton,

Ed Kaihatsu, Ray Podder, Jason Rogers, Michael Caito, Ridgely Goldsborough, Ron Blair, Tom Moyer.

ABOUT THE AUTHOR

JAMIE DOURAGHY's *Why* is to contribute to a greater good in all aspects of life. He does this as an executive coach, team facilitator, and founder of Life Work Integration, an organization that guides others to discover the *Why*, *How*, and *What* that drives them to succeed in life and work. Jamie has an MA from Syracuse University, is a certified CliftonStrengths Coach, a TEDx speaker, and a graduate of EO's Global Leadership Academy and Leadership Los Angeles. Jamie lives and fences in Los Angeles, and works with entrepreneurs and entrepreneurial teams globally to discover their own Why Stack and strengths. He's been married to his wife Katty for twenty-five years, and believes in the freedom that an integrated life brings.